LAND THAT JOB

MOVING FORWARD AFTER COVID19

SHARON DAVEY

Copyright (C) 2021 Sharon Davey

Layout design and Copyright (C) 2021 by Next Chapter

Published 2021 by Next Chapter

Cover art by CoverMint

Back cover texture by David M. Schrader, used under license from Shutterstock.com

Mass Market Paperback Edition

All rights reserved. No part of this book may be reproduced or transmitted in any form or by any means, electronic or mechanical, including photocopying, recording, or by any information storage and retrieval system, without the author's permission.

ALSO BY SHARON DAVEY

Awesome Careers for Gen Ys: easy strategies to create an amazing career & life, 2015, Global Publishing, Australia

DISCLAIMER

All the information, techniques, skills, and concepts contained within this publication are of the nature of general comment only and are not in any way recommended as individual advice. The intent is to offer a variety of information to provide a broader range of choices now and into the future, recognising that we all have widely diverse circumstances and viewpoints.

Should any reader choose to make use of the information contained herein, this is their decision, and the contributors (and their companies), authors and publishers do not assume any responsibilities whatsoever under any condition or circumstances. It is recommended that the reader obtain their own independent advice.

*This book is dedicated to my siblings, Jenny, Bill and Julie, and their partners, John, Jin Zhu and Peter. They have always been supportive of me during my career and proud that I am sharing my knowledge through my writing.
I am deeply grateful to them all.*

ACKNOWLEDGMENTS

Firstly, I want to acknowledge all of the people who have come to me over the years for assistance with their careers and job search activities. It was an honour and a privilege to work with you.

I also appreciate the opportunities that I was given to interview job seekers from various employers in my career. Being on that side of the table taught me a great deal.

There are many, many people I could thank but I have chosen to write a blanket thank you to anyone who has liked my posts on Facebook and other social media platforms, given me a kind word by text or messenger, or called me to wish me well. I appreciate every one of you. Thank you.

I have worked with many top class careers counsellors in my career. I particularly want to thank one of them. Jackie Rothberg, Director at the Career Action Centre in Melbourne, has been incredibly supportive of me over the years, and it has been my pleasure to have worked alongside her on several occasions. I appreciate her integrity, extensive knowledge of career education, and her loyal friendship.

Thank you, also, to Veronica Schwarz, fellow author and educationalist. Veronica is a dynamic and intelligent woman who has provided me with the opportunity to talk through many topics, including careers and job search, and the recommendation to approach Next Chapter to publish my books.

Thank you to the team at Next Chapter for your help and encouragement. I am delighted with our partnership.

Lastly, I want to thank my daughters, Jannine and Alison, son-in-law, John, and my grandson, Nicholas, for your unwavering love and support. Without you, my life would not be so rich and full. I am deeply grateful to all four of you.

FREE ARTICLES

Sharon has produced three free articles for specific jobseekers, that are designed to be read in conjunction to the material contained in *Land that Job: moving forward after Covid19*.

If you are interested in receiving one or more of these articles, email her on landthatjobaftercovid19@gmail.com and she will send them to you.

1. **Your first job: for those jobseekers with little or no experience in the workforce. Practical information about the basics.**
2. **Using your experience: helpful tips for the 50+ jobseeker. Looking at options and providing targeted strategies.**
3. **Starting your own business: Useful information and links to a range of sites that can help you get started. Statistics and down-to-earth suggestions to help you get started.**

A life lived in fear is a life half lived.

BAZ LUHRMANN, AUSTRALIAN
DIRECTOR, WRITER AND
PRODUCER

FOREWORD

The global pandemic that swept the world in 2020 disrupted many lives and caused a great deal of grief to many families. Businesses were all impacted. Some of them had to temporarily close their doors and lay off staff, a few flourished, many had to change the way they operated and, sadly, some went under. Small businesses were often particularly vulnerable because they didn't have the cash reserves to weather out the months of uncertainty, lockdown and the continued demands for rent from landlords.

Large numbers of people became unemployed, many for the first time in their lives. This is just one of the reasons that we have seen an increase in the numbers of people with poor mental health.

Young people didn't have the opportunities they once had to get their foot into the workforce by taking on casual jobs in hospitality and retail industries. If they were about to start, or had just started, a professional role, that was quickly taken away from them as the impact of the pandemic hit businesses hard.

People in the 50+ age bracket were another group that was significantly impacted. The initial job losses hit older workers harder, they were rehired more slowly, and even now, older workers continue to lose jobs more quickly than their slightly younger colleagues.

There was an increase in the numbers of people starting small businesses in 2020, across many Western countries. This probably arose from the frustration that workers felt about not having a job, and that when times are tough, people look for alternative pathways to earn an income.

As a result of the pandemic, reliance on digital technology for everyday life increased significantly and it has become more sophisticated. Along with that, many people have become more sophisticated users of technology, whether they wanted to or not! The nature of digital technology is that it expands and changes exponentially so its use will become even more entrenched in our lives into the future.

The long-term effect of the pandemic is likely to felt for some years, especially in industries that were severely impacted by the pandemic, such as in the travel and arts industries. Even those industries that are still operating are changing their structures and systems. Very few businesses will be untouched by the pandemic.

One of the changes that is still in flux and transition, at the time of writing this book, is the probable permanent change that will occur around employees working from home for at least part of the week. Many people enjoyed the flexibility of working from home, while being no less productive in their job roles. Some, of course, couldn't wait to get back to their normal environment because they missed the social aspect of working with others.

For some of us, working from home has led to seeking a sea or tree change. Many people are looking to change their lifestyles.

During times of lockdown, people had the opportunity to reflect on what was truly important to them and some are in the process of making big changes to their lives, post-Covid19.

This book is aimed at helping people make those changes in relation to their work lives. Hopefully, it will also challenge you to look differently at applying for jobs and going through the selection process. I would love it if more jobseekers come to see the whole process as less scary and much more do-able.

There are two elements that are particularly important in the post-pandemic world of job search and applying for jobs: technology, and connection with others. We will use technology to apply for jobs, and sometimes to be interviewed for them, too.

We may find job advertisements online BUT that is still likely to remain a smaller percentage than the jobs we find through our connections with others. Some of you may disagree with that statement but Covid19 showed us how much we valued others in our lives and so, for most people, our friends and family have become even more important than they were before. It is through them that we will hear or read about job opportunities or links to jobs, businesses, or industries.

There are many tips and strategies for your job search and job application process in this book and it is my fervent wish that it helps many people. I know that the vast majority of people want to be working, not just to pay the rent or put food on the table, but because they want to make a contribution or make a difference in the world.

Let this book help you do that!

But before we start, I want to bring you some words from a previous prime minister of Australia that might give you some indication of my writing style and approach.

> Those of you who have spent time with Australians know that we are not given to overstatement. By nature, we are laconic speakers and by conviction, we are realistic thinkers.
>
> JLIA GILLARD, PRIME MINISTER OF AUSTRALIA 2010-2013

I am realistic, down-to-earth and practical. I am not given to overstatement so if I emphasise something, you will know that I think that it's important. I also have a very Australian sense of humour so if it has snuck in, (and you're from another country), please forgive me.

Sharon Davey

INTRODUCTION

This book is aimed at getting you into the job you want. I have scanned or read through thousands of job applications over the years. I have sat in both the interviewer and interviewee seat many times. I have seen the mistakes that people often make on both sides of the table. I have written this book to help job applicants have a better chance of success, especially in this post-Covid19 era.

THE JOB SEARCH GAME

> Most people get stressed out by the thought of searching for a job. They don't realise, or they forget, that it's a game, a game that anyone can win.
>
> SHARON DAVEY, AUTHOR, CAREERS COACH

I understand that job search has a serious side, but people sometimes give it more heaviness than it deserves. I suggest that you put aside those serious thoughts, your fears and your pessimism, and tackle your job search with a different mindset. Come at it from a different perspective.

For a start, think of it as a 'numbers game'.

The more applications (good quality applications) you submit, the closer you'll get to obtaining a great job. Simple. Yes, even in the post-Covid19 world.

But it will not work if you put the same application in for every job. You've probably heard somebody say, "I've put in 200 applications and never got an interview". To me, that's like saying "I've banged my head against this brick wall 200 times and it still hurts". That's crazy!

There are two different sets of skills involved in job search.

The first set of skills is the written part. The second set of skills relates to the interview. Both sets of skills can be learnt. You can even become really good at them.

If you have sent off over ten applications without getting an interview, you need to review your written application. There will be ways it can be improved. This book will show you how.

If you keep getting interviews as a result of your applications, congratulations. You're obviously getting the written part right.

But if you keep getting interviews but not getting a job, you need to improve your skillset for that aspect of the process. <u>There will be ways to improve your interview performance.</u> Again, the tips, strategies and suggestions in this book will help you.

Please keep in mind that the job search game is not personal - so don't take it personally if you don't get offered a job. More on that later.

BUT FIRST, DO THIS

I'm going to start the book by suggesting that you stop thinking of employment in terms of job titles and start looking at it in terms of using the skills you've learnt, the attributes that you have, and the values that you hold. That could be a harder shift than you think.

However, given the changes that have taken place within traditional job roles, the emergence of new industries (and the demise of others), the importance of technology in today's work-place, and the rapid increase in the number of brand new job roles, it doesn't make sense to just apply for the jobs we've always applied for or in the places we have always applied for them.

We will also need to be clear about what we've got to offer as new job roles emerge and we consider whether we have at least some of the skills to do them.

Covid19 gave many people an opportunity to think about their career, whether they liked it or not! It has also given you an opportunity to change direction, if you want to. For some people, the change in direction will have arisen from reflecting that they could do something even bigger or more advanced in their current work environment. For others, the enforced slowdown gave them a chance to think about their lifestyles and what they really wanted their life to be like. And that might be about them trying something completely different that's more in line with what their heart is telling them to do.

Whatever has prompted us to consider a new direction, it makes sense for us to be very clear about what we have to offer an employer so that we can apply for a much broader range of jobs than we have done in the past. Those jobs won't necessarily be called what we have been used to, even if we are using the same skill set.

Now, the problem is that most people I've met in life don't have any idea of the breadth and number of their skills, attributes and values. I wish I had ten bucks for everyone who's ever told me "I haven't got many skills". It simply isn't true, for anyone. It isn't true about YOU.

In my first book, *Awesome Careers for Gen Ys: easy strategies to create an amazing career & life*, I created a table that went over eight pages or so that detailed the skills that young people use just doing everyday things. If I tried to do that for people who were 40+, it would take up a lot more pages because our skill set increases as we get older.

In the appendices to this book, you will find lists of skills, personal attributes, and values, plus adjectives and adverbs to support your written job application. You will be able to identify and then use some of the skills and attributes within your resumes.

It's a good idea to be clear about your values when you're considering what companies you'd like to work for and in case you are asked about them during the interview phase of a job application.

> Open your arms to change but don't let go of your values.
>
> DALAI LAMA, SPIRITUAL LEADER

THERE'S NOT JUST ONE PLACE TO LOOK FOR JOBS

If you want to apply broadly and go beyond advertised positions – and you really, really do need to do that - I will also show you how to target your applications vs taking a scatter gun approach. You'll learn where to send applications, where not to send them and how to use the online application process to your advantage.

A LinkedIn expert I know, Sharon Luxford, has kindly written a section of this book on how to use LinkedIn for excellent results.

Studies have shown that most people – somewhere around 80% - get jobs using their contacts. They can be personal or professional networking contacts. It's a strategy that works - and you will learn lots of ways to make it work well for you.

THE WRITTEN PART OF YOUR APPLICATION

In this section you will learn the dos and don'ts of resume writing, application letters and responding to key selection criteria and even tips on the email you send it all off with. I'll provide a few examples to help you get started.

Just remember that your written application must be proof-read – by you and at least one other person. I have seen thousands of resumes over my career and only about 10% of them were free of mistakes. It is important because employers will make assumptions about you, your attention to detail, your intelligence and your character but, most importantly of all, they will make assumptions about how well you will represent them as an employee. I get excited about seeing a resume that doesn't have any mistakes, (and that's a bit sad really).

There are ways to have your cover letter work for you and you'll hear me say 'never send the same cover letter for every application' and tell you why.

I have rarely seen people respond well to key selection criteria and I'd love to change that around. Please read that section through several times and apply the principles I give you. It will make a BIG difference.

> Essentially, making it as easy as possible for an employer or recruiter to absorb the information that you provide will help you on your way to getting that job.
>
> SHARON DAVEY, AUTHOR, CAREERS COACH

THE INTERVIEW

The key factor for performing well in an interview lies in your preparation for it.

You will learn how to answer the most commonly asked questions as well as some that are a bit tricky. If you've worked out what you're going to say beforehand – and practised your answers aloud – your level of confidence for at least 80% of the interview will be good or even very good. I made sure that I included tips to get over the nerves that many of you experience during interviews.

Another aspect of the interview process that can work for you or against you are the actions you take after the interview. Give yourself an advantage by handling this part of the process professionally.

THE APPENDICES

Lists and exercises, helpful advice and links to my YouTube videos, the appendices are – like the rest of the book – designed to help you get into work and move forward after Covid19.

OVERALL

There are many, many tips and strategies throughout the book that have come from my own experience of sitting on both sides of the table. I want you to get a job, so, whoever you are, at whatever age you're at, take on at least a few of the strategies and make a difference to your success rate.

> There are no secrets to success. It is the result of preparation, hard work and learning from failure.
>
> COLIN POWELL, AMERICAN STATESMAN

CHAPTER ONE

YOUR ATTITUDES AND BELIEFS ABOUT JOB SEARCH

ATTITUDES AND BELIEFS: A VERY IMPORTANT ELEMENT IN THE WHOLE PROCESS!

Throughout my years of helping people move from one job to another, or getting their first job, I have been surprised and saddened at the number of people who tell themselves that they wouldn't be able to get the job they really want (even if they're qualified to do it). They have usually listened to the voice inside their head that tells them that they are too old, too young, not experienced enough, not qualified enough, not good enough, not smart enough, not dynamic enough, or 'not' something or 'too' something else. They have listened to what the media says about young people or mature people or the labour market. They have taken on board what their mother / father / uncle / teacher / supervisor / peers said about them and their abilities.

They have become locked into a way of thinking about themselves (their gender, their age, their experience) or about what they have heard on the nightly news about the job market or what they have read on the internet somewhere.

And, right now in this almost post-Covid19 world, the outer and inner voices are sprouting doom and gloom all over the place. We know that it is going to be competitive out there. There's no hiding from that. We should also remind ourselves that economies do recover, entrepreneurial types will start businesses and employ people, and some businesses will even grow during disasters, and afterwards.

A competitive jobs market means that it is likely that you'll have to apply for more jobs before you're successful, and that can be dispiriting and exhausting. However, people still get new jobs, even in this sort of environment. This book will show you how you can make the most of what you have to offer and become more effective in the job application process.

Firstly, though, I think that it's important to look at the impact of what we listen to, whether it's from our friends, relatives or the nightly news OR whether it's what we're telling ourselves. If it's negative, it's not going to do us any favours at all. I know that it's not going to be easy to ignore the negativity but it's a necessity if you want to get a job.

In the post-Covid19 period, it will be tempting to think that you need to stick with the sort of job you've always had. However, you don't have to do that unless you want to do that.

People often apply for jobs on the basis of what they think they 'should' apply for or what they think is reasonable/acceptable given their qualifications, age, experience or gender.

They have developed a fixed mindset. It's usually fear-based and negative.

Effective job search requires a flexible mindset. If you can throw in creativity, fun and courage you will have a mindset that will lead you to many employment possibilities.

If you are willing to keep your mind open during the job search process – and take on board the suggestions that I make – in a spirit of fun and adventure rather than one of pessimism and/or deadly seriousness, you will be surprised at how quickly it will all fall into place for you.

If you are operating from a place of limitation, of fixed ideas, of uber seriousness, of fear (of something, anything), your job search will be much harder than it needs to be.

"Whether you think you can, or you think you can't – you're right".

HENRY FORD

A LITTLE MORE ABOUT LIMITING BELIEFS

If your patterns of belief and behaviour have, at the base, that:

- Life is hard and difficult
- You're not worthy
- You can't have what you really want
- No-one listens to you
- You're an outsider
- Or some other thought that you made up about yourself or life. It may have been adopted from your parents or other significant people, when you were a child.

You are likely to find the job search process difficult or hard; will tend to take any rejections personally; or will make it mean something negative about you or the world we live in.

You will do this even when the evidence that is there in front of you that you have:

- Been successful in the past (in getting a job and keeping it)
- A great skill set
- Been a valued employee for various companies
- At least basic literacy and numeracy
- At least a couple of people who like or love you

You will ignore or discount your own growth, qualifications and experience and convince yourself that some external factor is to blame or, worse still, that it's your own fault that this is happening to you.

I challenge you to identify your own limiting beliefs, and work on reducing their power over you, so that you can transform your experience with job search.

Whatever the voice inside your head is saying, it's at the base of your limiting beliefs about yourself and your world. Over time, the limiting beliefs even develop in their sophistication and become more layered, so much so that it seems more complicated than it is.

You have a decision to make.

Do you intend to keep these limiting beliefs and keep giving away your power to them, or is it time to acknowledge their existence and then send them packing?

I'm not going to pretend that it will all be fixed and that you'll get rid of your limiting beliefs instantly. It will take work, a willingness to take a 'good, hard look at yourself' and a willingness to make the necessary changes to the way you think and act, over and over. Your limiting beliefs built up over time and, while it won't take the same amount of time to dismantle them, they have been part of 'you' for some time and will take time to lessen their grip on you.

I acknowledge that, sometimes, it is a challenge to take responsibility for our thoughts and beliefs. It is easier to blame something outside of ourselves for our woes. The media is great at presenting the world as a difficult place, one where people have lots of hardships and where unexpected terrible events can happen to regular people. Within that context, it is easy to fall into the view that we have little control over our lives and that the world, including the world of work, is difficult and perhaps is even conspiring against us.

I want you to be able to cast aside any negative thoughts in relation to job search (and perhaps stop watching the nightly news) and focus now on the two skill sets I spoke about earlier. A reminder: the first skill set is the written part of your application, and the second is on the skills you use in your interview.

> Over time, we amass limiting beliefs about how life supposedly is – beliefs that are not valid. Then we allow these limiting beliefs to stop us from fully living our happiest lives.
>
> *KAREN SALMANSOHN, BEST-SELLING AUTHOR*

CHAPTER TWO

GETTING SMART ABOUT WHERE TO LOOK FOR JOBS

THERE'S NO ONE PLACE TO LOOK FOR JOBS

Some job seekers go straight to seek.com or careerone.com to look for jobs without realising that there are a whole lot of other job search options out there where the marketplace isn't quite so crowded with applicants.

When you remember that job search is a numbers game, the thing to do is to increase the numbers of positions for which you apply. One way of doing that is to have many irons in the fire. Just applying through these online recruitment services can severely limit your chances of success.

I will say this several times in the book – NEVER EVER EVER apply for just one job, wait to see how you go, find out you didn't get it, and then start looking again. That's a very inefficient and completely demoralising way to approach job seeking.

Apply for lots of jobs from lots of sources and you will always know there are other possibilities for you.

Aim at creating momentum in your job search. At any one time have at least eight job applications in progress. If you're sitting in an interview, knowing that you have another interview to attend, three applications you've just submitted, and three more to write, how do you think you'll feel? There will be an aura about you that tells the prospective employer that you have confidence, energy, initiative and positivity. You won't appear to be desperate or anxious – not good emotions in a job interview.

Sure, go to seek.com or indeed.com (or whatever are the most common job-seeking sites in your part of the world) but also try these other places as well.

DIRECT TO THE COMPANY OR ORGANISATION

Work out what companies you'd like to work for and then go directly to the business itself.

Look under the Employment, Careers or Jobs tab on their website. They may also have some articles or documents about what you need to know if you're applying for a job there. Don't assume that you know what they're saying because you've applied for jobs before. Check out their information because there could be some helpful advice that they've included to help job seekers.

Another reason for looking at that information is that they may include some step or snippet to test job applicants. For example, they might suggest that you read their values statement before applying so that you can determine whether your values match theirs. Then, in the subsequent interview, they might ask a question on your shared values. If you haven't 'done your homework', you will find yourself floundering when you have to answer the question.

Look at their website thoroughly. Read their Mission Statement or Vision. See what projects they're involved in or what products they sell. Have they won any awards or commendations? Do they support any charities or even have their own charity? What can you learn about the company's origins and its staff?

<u>Remember that the job application process is a two-way process.</u> You need to check them out as much as they're checking you out. Their website should be a positive indication of who they are and what they stand for.

If the position you're applying for involves the responsibility for the company website, make sure you examine it in much greater detail. In fact, analyse it thoroughly because you are likely to be asked questions about its functionality and design in the interview. You won't come across in a positive light if you haven't taken much notice of the website's effectiveness in the preparation phase.

UNIVERSITY AND TAFE/COMMUNITY COLLEGE EMPLOYMENT SERVICES

Every university and TAFE/community college will have an employment service to help their students access part-time positions while they're studying AND will advertise full-time positions as the students are finishing their courses. Frankly, you'd be crazy not to access these services if you are a student. Some of these services, but not all, are offered to past students as well.

Some employers will prefer students from specific universities. This will be because the institution has produced high quality graduates from a particular academic area or that the university has had breakthrough results with the academic research they have carried out. Some will simply have a 'good name' for something, such as the engineers they produce.

As a student, always make sure that you know what research your faculty is involved in so that you can speak about it confidently in an interview, even once you've completed your course.

Most universities and TAFEs/community colleges actively seek strong industry links with employers so that they are able to offer both industry-based experience during courses as well as post-course employment options for their students. (There has been increasing pressure on higher education institutions to ensure students are 'work ready' when they finish courses so having strong links to industries and quality employers satisfies the needs of all parties).

INDUSTRY SPECIFIC RECRUITMENT AGENCIES

The hospitality industry is a typical example of an industry specific employment area. Hospitality is a field that often requires staff who have specific experience and so employers will list jobs with a hospitality recruitment agency to 'weed out' anyone who doesn't have the background they want.

A few examples in Australia are:

www.frontlinerecruitmentgroup.com/hospitality

www.hospitalityrecruitment.com.au

flexistaff.com.au

The same principle applies with other industry specific agencies so use your favourite search engine to check out what's available within your field.

SPECIALIST EMPLOYMENT SERVICES

These are similar to industry specific agencies. However, they may offer employment across industries. Jobs in the not-for-profit sector and the apprenticeship sector are often across industries, professional fields or regions, but share a common thread.

For example, employers in the not-for-profit sector often seek out potential employees who understand the particular benefits and challenges of working in that sector; have a history of working with disadvantaged people; and whose values are aligned with theirs.

A few examples in Australia are:

www.nfpjobs.com.au

au.indeed.com

www.australianapprecticeships.gov.au

FEDERAL AND STATE GOVERNMENT EMPLOYMENT

Federal and state governments are often required to advertise their positions on official websites and/or in a newspaper.

Applications for government jobs usually involve having to address key selection criteria as well as having to submit targeted resumes and a formal application letter. Please make sure that you read the section in this book on responding to key selection criteria.

Because government job applications can be quite time consuming, I usually suggest that interested parties call the person whose name is listed on the position description as the contact. You have an opportunity to ask about the job PLUS find out if someone has been in or acting in the position for some time.

Some government jobs must be advertised every three or five years. If you know that someone has been in the role or acting in it for at least 12 months, it would be worth asking if that person is likely to be re-applying for the position. While you might not be given that information, it would be worth you considering whether you want to go to the trouble of applying for a job that could well be ear-marked (unofficially) for someone else.

I once saw a job for a senior role in a regulatory body (semi-government) listed in the hospitality section of a newspaper. It was not a hospitality job. The advertisement was only a couple of lines but had met the government requirement of being placed in the newspaper! I suppose it saved a lot of people from wasting their time in applying for the position, but it did seem a bit cynical to me.

LOCAL GOVERNMENT

While these jobs are often advertised in other places online and in the press, the individual local government/ council websites are the best place to look, especially if you want to work close to your home. Save the website in your favourites and check it on a weekly basis to see if any new jobs have been listed there.

If you are particularly keen on working in local government, you could establish positive professional relationships with local government personnel by attending business breakfasts they run or by being on local committees within your area of expertise. These strategies could mean that you hear about roles that will be advertised. Being 'known' will certainly improve your chances of being selected for an interview if you choose to apply for a job with that organisation.

LOCAL NEWSPAPERS

Even though there aren't a lot of truly local newspapers anymore and even fewer jobs in them, the employers advertising there are often hoping that they will pick up a local person for their role. When people don't have to travel a long way to get to their job, they often stay in the position longer. For some jobs, local knowledge is useful.

So, grab your local newspaper when it's delivered and see if there are any possibilities there for you.

VOLUNTEERING, INDUSTRY PLACEMENTS, AND INTERNSHIPS

Many people do not realise that unpaid work in Australia is illegal. While it is legal for a prospective employer to ask you to work a trial shift, it is generally only be for a limited time and only in order for an employer to check that you have the required skills.

Volunteer work and internships are legal but are governed by strict rules.

Go to fairwork.gov.au for further details. If you suspect that you are being exploited, the information on that site will clarify the situation for you.

VOLUNTEERING

Working as a volunteer through an organisation's volunteer program is a useful – and legal - way of gaining or adding to your skill set. It's also an opportunity for those people, who have years of experience and many skills, to further contribute to society. Many not-for-profit organisations have volunteer programs and some of them offer meaningful work that can develop and/or utilise your skills.

Volunteering is usually seen favourably by employers who like the fact that you have not just been sitting around waiting for a job to fall in your lap but have been contributing to others. It also demonstrates that you have initiative and a good work ethic.

I suggest that you list your volunteer experience(s) in with your paid employment because it is part of your work history. It has a validity of its own.

CREATING YOUR OWN VOLUNTEER EXPERIENCE

Two of the young people I interviewed while I was writing *Awesome Careers for Gen Ys: easy strategies to create an amazing career and life* suggested taking a more deliberate and planned approach to creating a valuable volunteering experience. They suggested researching a couple of not-for-profit organisations to see what they might need done but might not be able to afford. They said that it made sense to put forward a proposal of one-two pages outlining your idea and how you could use your skills to make it happen.

An example of this might be a proposal that you put forward to your local tennis club to set up and write a monthly blog for them that you would send out to members. If they aren't on Facebook, you could suggest creating a page for the club and putting up photos of matches and tournaments to create interest in their activities. The underlying aim might be to increase membership of the club.

INDUSTRY PLACEMENTS

These are part of college and university courses and are an excellent way to build up your skills, create links with people within the industry you want to become part of, and even possibly to be offered a job. Never approach an industry placement as just one of the requirements of a course. Opportunities often emerge from them. It may not happen in the short term, but a future opportunity could arise through a contact you make.

If it is possible to do more than one industry placement, do it! It will give you the chance to increase your skill set plus the opportunity to make more contacts in your industry. That's a win-win.

INTERNSHIPS

Unpaid internships (or work experience) are OK if it's a student/vocational placement; or

there's no employment relationship. For more specific information on internships and what constitutes an employment relationship, please go to fairwork.gov.au.

Gaining an internship can be useful in gaining experience, knowledge of the sector you've chosen as your career, and for making connections. They can sometimes lead to obtaining a job.

In Australia, companies that take on interns will be very mindful of the Fair Work Act, and most will adhere to the rules and principles of the Act. If, however, you take up an internship and subsequently believe that you're being exploited, contact fairwork.gov.au to get advice about your next step.

> The successful man (or woman) will profit from his/her mistakes and try again in a different way.
>
> DALE CARNEGIE, AMERICAN AUTHOR, LECTURER

CHAPTER THREE

LINKEDIN BROUGHT TO YOU BY SHARON LUXFORD, LINKEDIN EXPERT

I met Sharon Luxford at a conference. It didn't take long before we were chatting about tools that people use to get work. Of course, Sharon spoke to me about LinkedIn. I have come to a greater understanding of the power of this great platform as a result of her knowledge and stories.

(Of course, I now regularly revise my LinkedIn profile. I suggest that you do that, too).

Sharon generously agreed to write about LinkedIn for this book. If you'd like to connect with her and ask her to help you with your profile, there is an offer in the back of this book that you can access.

Now, on to Sharon's words about LinkedIn…

LINKEDIN

Imagine you are driving down a long highway and there are billboards along the side of the road. Grey billboard after grey billboard with no photos or headlines to momentarily grab your attention on the long journey you are on.

Then suddenly there's a billboard with a photo of someone smiling down at you and a couple of words that grab your attention. Let me clarify here that you are the passenger in this imaginary vehicle on this imaginary highway. The driver's eyes are on the road, focussed on getting you both safely to the business networking event you are attending to meet new people and expand your online and offline (in real life) professional network.

Anyhoo, back to the story…

This magnificent billboard stands out like a beacon in the night, compared to all the others. There is a photo of a real person and words that in your brief glance, seem to align with the person in the photo on this colourful and lively billboard.

The moral of this imaginary story is: If you don't have a photo or head shot and an authentic and meaningful headline on your LinkedIn Profile then you may be being perceived as one of the grey billboards that people will pass by, without remembering who you are, where you met or what you do or could do for them. Sad, huh.

If you want to remain a grey billboard in the highway of life, then probably best that you stop reading right here and skip to the next section of this book, as the remainder of my section is going to give you some rock-solid reasons to be 'seen on LinkedIn' and explain how to help you to STOP BEING A GREY BILLBOARD!!

And in the years of 2020, 2021 and beyond, having an attention-grabbing online presence has never been more important, as much of the world went home and online, for work, job seeking, entertainment and connection, as many of us were in lockdown and could not travel…even to work.

Congratulations to those of you still with me…you have taken the very brave step to begin to utilise the **FREE PERSONAL BRANDING PLATFORM** that is LinkedIn and I commend you on taking action. So, let's get you started…

ABOUT YOUR PHOTO

From the previous paragraphs and expanding on the 'billboard analogy', I hope you have gleaned that a photo of you or a head shot, as they are commonly called , is an ESSENTIAL first step to being seen on LinkedIn.

There are however some rules or things you should consider before you start flicking through your phone to find that photo from your best friend's wedding, where you had the opera glasses props and were doing a high kick, that showed just a little too much...you.

The photo must be of YOU. Your face. Ideally smiling and I cannot stress this enough...HOW YOU LOOK...NOW!! We all have those favourite pics where we looked fabulous at our high school or university graduation, when we got married or 5-10 years ago. Let's face it, we all looked younger...when we were...younger.

In my opinion and from my experience, which is the source of this whole section, none of these pics are suitable options for your LinkedIn head shot. If you don't want to go to the expense of having a professional head shot done, ask a friend to take a photo of you against a light background, when you are in your usual work clothes. Take a few shots and pick the best one and upload it to your LinkedIn Profile and you're done. Simples!!

A word of warning here, if you are going to do some 'serious work' on your LinkedIn Profile, please **TURN YOUR NOTIFICATIONS OFF**. This will spare your network seeing numerous notifications about small updates to your profile. How to do this can change, so best my advice is to Google "how do I turn off LinkedIn notifications" and select the response provided by LinkedIn. I use this method for any questions I have about LinkedIn to ensure I have the most current instructions about how to do anything on LinkedIn.

YOUR HEADLINE & A LIGHT BULB MOMENT

Your Headline usually defaults to your Job Title, which can be ok…if you have a job title that meaningfully explains what you 'actually do' then it's probably an okay option. I encourage you to think about any billboard you have ever seen. They mostly have some kinda catch phrase or 'elevator pitch' which is a compelling statement about the brand. On LinkedIn 'the brand' we are talking about and promoting is…YOU!!

Let me explain by way of a 'real life' example, which also includes a 'light bulb' moment that changed how I thought about LinkedIn. I was attending a networking event in Sydney, Australia. The purpose was to hear the guest speaker who, was for a time to become my LinkedIn Mentor.

The headline part of the story goes like this. I had just introduced myself to a woman who said, "My name is Anna and I'm an accountant". I asked her what kind of accountant, which she then explained. When the next person joined our group, I introduced Anna to them and said something like: "This is Anna. She helps business owners remain compliant with their tax and other obligations, allowing them to spend time with their clients and grow their business".

The person then asked with great interest "Wow… what do you do?" to which Anna responded, somewhat in disbelief, "I'm an accountant?". It was in that moment that Anna realised that she was far more than 'just an accountant'.

My light bulb moment for me, occurred during the guest speaker's presentation, when he said,

"LinkedIn is like a virtual networking event…are you only going to talk to people that you know?".

Up to that moment, I had treated LinkedIn as a 'private club', if I didn't know you…you didn't get in.

Yet there I was at a networking event, standing in a room of 25ish people that I didn't know, who were fast becoming people that I did know, and I began to wonder about the validity of my previous LinkedIn Connection Philosophy.

In that moment, I opened up my potential connections to either people I have met or profiles that (by my own pre-determined standards) I believe, are authentic and represent people I want in my network. There is no right or wrong here. Who you choose to accept or invite into your LinkedIn network is entirely up to what feels right for you at any given time. There are no specific rules, so make up your own that work for you.

YOUR SUMMARY

The Summary section is sometimes overlooked but is a fantastic opportunity to tell your story, sharing more about who you are and why you do, what you do. You can use your Summary to talk about not only what you do now but also what led you to the job or business you are in now. You have 2,000 character [including spaces and punctuation], so focus on what you want to say and then edit as needed to make it fit. Write your draft in a Word doc or something with a character count and when you're satisfied, add it to your LinkedIn Summary. Always double check the character count.

Whilst it sounds quite simple, this can sometimes be a very daunting task and, along with crafting an attention-grabbing headline, is one of the main reasons that people come to me, to help them create a professionally written LinkedIn Profile. I encourage you to give it a go and if it all becomes too hard, you'll find an offer in the back of this book that may help you take the next step to making your LinkedIn profile stand out.

YOUR SKILLS

You know you have skills, even if you can only think of a few to start with. LinkedIn allows you to add up to 50 skills to your profile and I strongly recommend that you use all of them.

Start with your resume, look over your current job description and some recent job ads for your kind of role and begin making a list. If you're really stuck, LinkedIn has a dropdown menu that can help you. Once you've got your list of skills, add them to your LinkedIn profile. You can prioritise as you go or once you're done. You can now be endorsed for these skills by your connections (people in your LinkedIn network).

There is also a list of skills and attributes (and the difference between them) at the end of this book, that may also help you. 'Cause that's the purpose of this book…to help you present the best version of yourself online, when you are looking for a new job, or considering a career change.

YOUR EDUCATION & EXPERIENCE

Key points to follow for adding your Education to your profile are accuracy and timeline. Make sure you have the exact name of your qualification and the institution you attended. You can also include some details about the qualification, such as a brief outline of what the course covered. Remember that you may be an expert in your qualification, but the person reading your profile may not be.

Your Experience should cover your job title, where you worked and your start and finish dates. In the free text section include a short sentence about your employer and what they do, a summary of your role and any key achievements and responsibilities. Browse your resume for these and spend some time thinking about each role in an objective and reflective manner, to critically assess what you did well and describe these using headings and dot points for ease of reading.

IN CLOSING...

I could write about LinkedIn and how powerful this free personal branding platform can be to help you elevate your online presence, which in turn supports your presence offline or 'in real life', for hours. Alas, the word count prevails, and I must close this section, so you can move onto the next exciting and valuable piece of job seeking and job applications.

Please do consider spending some time rereading these words and as you work on your LinkedIn Profile. You may even learn something about yourself, which in turn may just be the thing that helps you stand out and get that next job, make that next great connection, or find your perfect client.

I wish you success in your career endeavours and if you're in need of some further help with LinkedIn, there is an offer and my contact details at the end of this book.

Cheers and thank you for reading and please feel free to reach out and connect with me on LinkedIn.

Sincerely

Sharon Luxford

> If you can get better at your job, you should be an active member of LinkedIn, because LinkedIn should be connecting you to the information, insights and people to be more effective.
>
> REID HOFFMAN, AMERICAN INTERNET ENTREPRENEUR AND AUTHOR

CHAPTER FOUR

YOUR CONTACTS: YOUR MOST IMPORTANT RESOURCE

CONTACTS (YOUR NETWORK OF FRIENDS, ACQUAINTANCES, AND RELATIVES) HAVE ALWAYS BEEN THE MAIN SOURCE OF EMPLOYMENT FOR JOB SEEKERS.

Today, it's more important than ever. A recent survey conducted on LinkedIn found that 85% of people got their most recent job through the networks of people they already knew. This is consistent with many other surveys that show similar results.

The other important result of those surveys is that only 2-4% of people get a job from using online job boards (such as seek or indeed). That's not a big outcome in the overall picture so don't put all your time into looking for jobs that way. Spend 2-4% of your allocated job search time on job board sites but not much more than that.

You have a fantastic resource – your contact list – and it is right there under your nose. It is critical that you access your contacts and networks to help you get into employment quickly.

WHO COUNTS AS CONTACTS?

- Parents
- Friends
- Relatives
- Neighbours
- Former or current teachers or lecturers
- Past colleagues and work mates
- Past employers or bosses
- Past professional affiliates
- People you've met at networking events, business breakfasts, etc
- People you've met at conferences or workshops
- Your hairdresser, personal trainer, manicurist, massage therapist
- Your doctor, chiropractor, physiotherapist
- Sporting acquaintances, coaches, managers
- Church friends or acquaintances
- Anyone you've met at yoga, a concert, at a coffee shop, etc
- People at organisations where you've been a volunteer
- All your friends on Facebook, your contacts on LinkedIn, anyone you know on social media
- Basically, most people you've ever met (although not people who have been counselled by you)

DON'T BRUSH THIS IDEA OFF BECAUSE YOU THINK I MEAN THAT YOU WILL BE ASKING THESE PEOPLE FOR A JOB. THAT'S NOT WHAT I'M SAYING HERE. STAY WITH ME.

Many of the people you've met would have liked you and would be happy to help you out. We don't know who other people know, not their full range of contacts.

Your friends and acquaintances may know someone who would be very helpful to you and your job search, but they won't know unless you tell them what you're looking for and what you need.

So, right now, before you go on reading, create your list. Don't leave anyone off. Put everyone you know on it. This could take a while, but it will be worth it.

A WORD OF CAUTION

Don't think of or treat your contacts and networks as walking job leads. If you haven't seen them for a while, you need to re-establish your connection with them. You can be open about looking for work but don't make your interaction with them just about that.

Many people have re-established contacts with others during this Covid19 era, so it won't be odd for you to reach out to say, 'hello, I was just thinking about you'.

If it comes up naturally, you can ask them for advice about where you should look for work or whether they have heard of any openings coming up at their organisation or with a competitor. Doing it that way takes the pressure off them and allows them to be helpful.

WHAT TO SAY TO YOUR CONTACTS WHEN YOU ARE LOOKING FOR A NEW JOB

There are two ways to go here. One is to simply ask your contact if they know anyone who needs a bookkeeper (or whatever your professional is) and the other is to be more general and state what problem you can solve for an employer.

Some examples of the problem-solving approach are:

- I'm great working with my hands and can fix/mend most things.
- I can establish rapport with anyone, regardless of their age, race, gender or sexual orientation and love to be of service to people.
- I'm good at creating and leading a cohesive team.
- I want to inspire and empower people to live their best lives.
- I am great at solving people's financial problems.
- I like to write simple, easy to understand answers to complex problems.
- I want to help organisations get their systems in order.

This approach requires you knowing what your main driver is and having a good understanding of your skills. Take a look at the skills list in Appendix A if you're not sure about yours.

It's really worthwhile creating a statement, like the ones I've written above, for yourself in this post-Covid19 era. Your 'usual' industry may be in a sustained down-turn but there are going to be industries out there that are looking for people with your skill set. It may not be the same context, but it will call on you to do what you do well anyway.

Taking this approach is likely to produce more results than asking if they know someone who needs a bookkeeper (or whatever).

A FOCUSSED APPROACH

There is no point in just saying to someone 'I'm looking for a new job' and expecting that they will know precisely what you're looking for or even the sort of work you'd be prepared to do. Even if it's someone you've worked with before, remind them again what it is that you're good at and what qualifications you have.

Don't be fixated on the job title. Ask if they know anyone who needs help with their BAS reports or getting their taxation documentation together. They might have a friend who'd complained to them about the issues they've had in getting their taxation documents sorted and, suddenly, here you are, providing the solution.

Be specific about what you want but avoid talking in jargon.

Another sentence to avoid saying is 'I'll do anything'. It really isn't useful or constructive and won't help someone who would genuinely like to help you.

Before you talk to your contacts and networks, make a list of the things you'd like to have in a new job, the sort of tasks you'd like to do and the skills that you like to use. Communicate that information to your contacts and networks - and you could find them coming up with suggestions for job roles that hadn't occurred to you.

A recent client of mine had worked mainly in criminal justice and corrections with young people. I was delighted that she had identified her skill set precisely and was, therefore, applying quite broadly for a range of positions. They included School-

Industry Liaison, Library Assistant roles, and Community Development work. I was pleased that she wasn't limiting herself to job titles that she had previously had but was expanding what was possible for her life and career.

HOW CAN YOUR CONTACTS HELP YOU?

Tell people how they can help you. Here are some ways they can do that:

- Give your name to their employer, formally, or just casually.
- Let you know when a job arises at their workplace, or if they see something on social media.
- Suggest places for you to make an application.
- Tell their friends and acquaintances about you.

Some organisations offer incentives for their staff to refer prospective employees to their HR department. The incentives might be simple, like a couple of tickets to the cinema, but others will have a monetary value attached to them.

The benefits to the business of doing this are that they will get to interview someone that is already valued by one of their staff, plus they don't have to advertise so extensively. The bottom line for the business is that both the risks and expenses associated with recruiting an unknown person are minimised.

UNSURE OF YOUR SKILLS?

Knowing your skills and which ones you most like to use is critical. How will you apply for the right job for you if you don't recognise what particular gifts you bring to the world?

Look at the Appendices section of this book to make lists of the things that you have, that you are and that you value. You are unique. No-one else has quite the same combined set of skills, attributes and values. The more you become aware of what it is that you have to offer, the better you can inform others about it and the easier it is for them to help you get what you want.

Highlight your top ten words in the Skills, Attributes and Values lists that best describe who you are and what you like to do. Use those words in your resumes, application letters and interviews.

If you are struggling with what to do next and you're thinking about a career change, you might like to download (for free) a worksheet I created years ago that has had a profound impact for many people who have completed it. It's called Your Ideal Work. If you would like me to email you a copy, please contact me at landthatjobaftercovid19@gmail.com and I will send it to you.

STRATEGIES FOR INCREASING YOUR NETWORKS

These are not in any order of importance, but I challenge you to try at least three of them.

Ask for a work reference

If you didn't do so when you left jobs you've had, contact your previous employer or supervisor and ask if they'd be willing to provide a verbal reference for you. It maintains the connections and could be useful for your job search. There may even be a chance of employment, even if it's just temporary or a short-term contract. If that's offered to you, say yes (unless you were treated poorly there, no job is worth a repeat of that).

Mini resume

Produce a mini 'resume' (just a one pager) that lists the things you're really good at including what problems you like to solve, your key attributes and a very brief <u>summary</u> of your past employment. Give copies of it to people who express interest in your job search. Always have a few copies in your briefcase or the boot of your car.

Business cards

Have a business card made up. You can usually have them made cheaply through Vistaprint.com or a similar business. On one side, have your name and about four aspects of your expertise. For example, Jemima Smith – Film, Video, Television, Sound. On the other side, put your name again, your qualifications and your contact details.

Make sure it's simple, stylish and not crowded with information. Hand them out to people wherever you go. It's amazing how many times I've used the information on business cards to contact people about potential job leads months after they've given them to me.

Give several cards each to your hairdresser, personal trainer or manicurist next time you go. Tell them what you're looking for and ask them to pass on your details to anyone they know who's in your field of expertise.

Conduct an informational interview

People are busy, but some will respond to a request for an informational interview that will only take ten minutes. Ask for ten minutes from them to provide you with some advice about career opportunities within their industry. <u>Tell them that you're not there to ask them for a job.</u>

Prepare some questions to ask them prior to the interview. The questions could be something like the following:

- Where would you look for employment within your industry?
- What sort of skills do you think are most important for people to have in your industry?
- Do people usually stay in your industry for a long time? (or what is the staff turnover like in your industry?)

- How did you get started in this industry?
- What advice would you give to someone wanting to get started in your industry now?

Ask the questions and then thank them very much for their time and end the conversation. Afterwards, send them a written note of thanks. Don't just send an email. Anyone can do that. They will remember the person who sent them a written thank you.

DO NOT ask them for a job and DO NOT take up more than the ten minutes you've asked for.

They are likely to have given you some invaluable information. Act on it!

Business Breakfasts or Seminars

Many local councils hold business breakfasts (or late afternoon seminars) every few months. It's worth paying the (usually) small cost to attend and meet people of all walks of life. Your focus here has to be on the people you're meeting. Ask them about themselves and their business, how they got started and what advice they would give to people wanting to get into the business.

Remember that the person asking the questions is the one in charge of the conversation - and the more you listen, the greater rapport you will establish. If you ask questions, be attentive as they answer and thank them as you leave them (handing them your business card as you go), and they will be left with a very favourable opinion of you.

Attending these events expands your network and puts your friendly, interested face in front of potential leads to employment - and you'll be learning things as well.

Professional Associations Events

When one of my nieces was job hunting, she attended professional development activities offered by her professional association. At that stage, she was not eligible for full membership, but she used the opportunity to meet people (read 'potential colleagues/employers') as well as expand her professional knowledge. As an associate member, you usually don't have to pay as much to attend such seminars so that's another bonus.

This is a good way for you to become better known in your field. Handing out your business card to people you meet is a legitimate way for you to expand your network and to establish yourself professionally.

Join alumni groups or organisations

Whether it's a school or university you attended, there are often alumni groups formed for the purpose of continuing the connection you all once had. Regardless of your personal experience there, the association will want to welcome you.

This is a good way to re-form friendships and develop new ones. Often, alumni associations will have created their own 'job boards' for their members to access. It's another way of sourcing jobs.

Join a service club

An excellent way of expanding your network – and doing a lot of good within your community – is to join Rotary or Lions Clubs. There are others, but these are the best known.

There is usually a good cross section of employers present at each meeting. Remember that employers know other employers. When they get to know you, they are potential sources of leads for employment.

Another great aspect to becoming a member of a service club is that they are involved in fundraising and events that contribute to the community. You will feel better about yourself plus it's a great thing to have on your resume.

Take a class or join Toastmasters

Doing something that interests you and builds your skills is good for your self-confidence if you haven't got back on your feet after Covid19. Obviously, you'll also be meeting a whole new set of people. We never know how many contacts that another person might have. Meeting them might just be the thing that turns your life around.

Toastmasters is a wonderful organisation and will be full of positive people, all wanting to improve their speaking skills and meeting up with other interesting people. They are very welcoming to newcomers.

Meet Ups

Another way of expanding your contacts and personal network is to join a Meet Up group. Go online and check out the Meet Up groups in your area. They are a great way to meet new people. Meet Up groups are formed for all sorts of purposes and you can even form one yourself. From social events to walking/hiking to learning about bitcoin, the range of Meet Up groups is endless. Explore what works for you and become a member of one or two groups.

This is one of the 'slow burn' approaches within your job search strategies because here you will be, first and foremost, working on establishing connections with a new group of people. In the initial stages, you would not talk about looking for a job, but as you form genuine friendships with people your job search activities would arise naturally in conversation.

Talk to people

Talk to people wherever you go, whether it's at your local coffee haunt, at the gym, on the train, wherever. If you think that this would be difficult, practice it in simple ways first. Rather than telling them about you, ask them something about themselves or comment on something they're doing.

For example, if you're browsing in the garden section at a hardware store and you notice someone with a trolley with lots of potting mix and a dozen plants, you could say, 'wow, looks like you've got a lot of work to do'. People are usually happy to be acknowledged and so are likely to reply with a friendly response.

Or if you're on the train and a muffled announcement comes over the loud-speaker, you could turn to a fellow traveller and ask, 'did you hear what they said?' You may not get as many friendly responses on the train because people get lost in their own little worlds but if you ask, with a smile, you are likely to get a positive response from them.

I've formed life-long friendships with people after I've stood in a queue to get into a concert. Most people love connecting with others so just talk to them. Have no expectations. Just connecting with someone else will make the day better for both of you.

What NOT to do

Don't put your discontent about your current job or situation up on Facebook or other forms of social media. Even if you think that your settings are really private, information may still be available that you don't want to make public.

It's not just your current employer and workmates that could judge you for your words of criticism. Many employers will routinely do a search of social media to gain a 'view' of their prospective employees. If you have criticised one employer online/publicly, you may do it to them, too. That will be a reason for them not to employ you.

Employers want you to be a positive representative for their company so make sure there are no photos of you on social media being high or drunk.

As well, don't appear to be desperate about your job search, even if you are. Don't be the person others avoid because all you do is talk about your need to get a job.

Stay in touch with your connections

After you've got your new job, keep in contact. If your contact had something to do with you getting your new job, consider taking them out for a meal or a coffee as a way of expressing your appreciation.

You might be able to 'pay it forward' for someone else or help your contact out in the future.

> The business of business is relationships; the business of life is human connection.
>
> ROBIN S SHARMA, CANADIAN AUTHOR OF THE MONK WHO SOLD HIS FERRARI BOOK SERIES

CHAPTER FIVE

BEING SMART ABOUT YOUR JOB SEARCH

A REMINDER...

It's not personal...

I have seen many job seekers become really stressed and suffer knockbacks to their self-confidence when they have not got an interview for a job for which they've applied.

They often make the mistake of thinking that there's something wrong with them. There's not!

The important thing to realise is that being selected – or not selected – for an interview (or for the job) is not personal. The recruiter/employer is NOT thinking 'this person is terrible'. They are not thinking about you as a person. They are considering whether you have what they think they need.

They may be looking for someone who is just like the person who has just left the job, or they might be looking for someone completely different. The point here is that there are sometimes unspoken things that the recruiter/employer is looking for and you will never know what those things are. Sometimes the employer may not even be aware of their own prejudices or beliefs.

At the first stage in the selection process, the recruiter/employer is just assessing your suitability for the job. They may have received anywhere from 10 to 500 applications and so their first assessment is quick and very analytical. It is not about you as a person. It is about them reducing the mass of applicants down to a manageable number so that they can decide who to interview. This is the reason why it's important that your written application is well structured, presents you and your skills and experience in the best light, and is free from mistakes.

Even if the employer rejects your application because of your poor spelling or grammar, it won't be personal, it won't be because they think <u>you</u> are crap. They might think your spelling or grammar is crap, but they will be more concerned about your ability to represent them in a professional way, in your written communication, rather than it being personal.

You may need to do some of the following:

- Approach your job search differently,
- Expand where you're sourcing potential jobs,
- Increase the number of jobs you're applying for,
- Become more skilled at analysing what the employer is looking for,
- Ask at least two people (preferably not from your own generation or ethnic group) to proof-read your applications. Having two people whose background is different will mean that they bring a different 'eye' to

your application. It's critical that your job applications are a Mistake-Free-Zone!
- Change (not necessarily by much) what you have written in your resume, your application letter or in your responses to the key selection criteria,
- Create your own list of interview questions before each interview and practice answering them out loud,
- Enlist the help of others when you're practising for your upcoming interviews,
- Prepare for your job interviews and stop flying by the seat of your pants,
- Change your mind-set about yourself, your age, your skillset, your location, the job market, your qualifications or about anything else that's getting in the way of your job search success.

The tweaking you may need to do may not be major (although sometimes it is) but it will be necessary if you want a different result.

TREAT YOUR JOB SEARCH LIKE A JOB!

If you want to be successful with your job search quickly, you need to do the following things:

- Read this book and take the suggestions on board,
- Be organised,
- Apply for jobs constantly,
- Allocate several hours every weekday towards your job search,
- Keep a diary – either on paper or on your smart phone.

Some people apply for a job, wait to see if they get an interview, get or don't get the interview and then wait again to see if they were successful. Sometimes they'll wait for weeks! Then they start the process again.

I have met with some people who have told me that they have been applying for jobs for six months. When I ask how many jobs they've applied for, they tell me they've applied for five. I say, "per week". They look startled and say, "no, five in six months".

I strongly suggest that you don't job search this way. In fact, forget the 'strongly suggest' part. **If you're serious about wanting a job, you MUST NOT job search this way**.

If you're serious about wanting a job, you MUST apply for lots of them. The more jobs you apply for, the more likely you'll get one quickly. You will have to follow the 'rules', formats and processes that I cover in this book but, if you do, your chances of getting a job quickly will significantly increase. Remember that job search is a numbers game. The more you apply for, the closer you get to success.

Think about it. If you're applying for lots of jobs and doing it well, you will have other 'irons in the fire' whenever you go for an interview. It will take the pressure off that specific interview because, even though you might quite like the idea of this particular job, it will be just one of a number of possible positions you'll be offered. And the more interviews you attend, the better you will get with your interview performance especially if you are prepared to learn from your experience.

I've noticed that when people use this very active method of job search, suddenly they find themselves being made several offers in the one week. I think it's because there is a different energy about them. They are more confident, self-assured, excited and positive. They walk into interviews in a more relaxed manner. They know that's only going to be a matter of time before they get a YES (or several of them at once) so their level of stress is reduced.

> For every minute spent organizing, an hour is earned.
>
> BENJAMIN FRANKLIN, A FOUNDING FATHER OF THE USA

GETTING ORGANISED

One of the things that will really help you will be organising your job search. If you're an organised type, you'll probably love the idea of spreadsheets to map out your job search. If not, you mightn't be thrilled by it, but you will come to find it useful. Link your spreadsheet to the calendar on your phone. Set up reminders so you don't forget your follow-up actions.

You need to keep records of what jobs you've applied for and when, the dates of the interviews, their outcomes and notes you've made about the company.

If you've sent off an application and haven't heard anything, making a follow up call a week after you've sent it or a week after you've had the interview is perfectly acceptable. But you do need to keep track of the dates of the activities related to that particular application.

It's a good idea to have notes because you don't want to forget or get confused about which place you did or didn't like when you went to the interview. Sometimes, an interviewer might mention another role that they will be recruiting for in a month or two's time. You might be interested because you liked the company and so you would make a note to contact them about that time.

Don't ever feel as if you're 'bothering' someone and that you shouldn't call to check on the progress of an application or to follow up after an interview. As long as you're not calling every day (make your call about a week after the interview), the employer or recruiter will just see you as someone who has initiative and who is being active in their job search.

Your Job Search Record spreadsheet might look something like this:

Business name & address	Business contact details	Role applied for	Date applied for	Result	Follow-up	Comments
ABC Insurance 79 High St, Bigtown	Susan Smith HR Manager 0412345678	Reception	24/9	Letter saying not successful	Sent thank you note 24/9 Called 6/10	Susan Smith said that I didn't have the sort of experience they wanted
Big Design 32 Mack St Bendigo	Ben Brown Director 59323232	Reception/ admin	25/9	Interview 5/10	Sent thank you note 25/9 Called 8/10	Ben said it was between me & another girl, but he gave her the job

You could add in other columns if you like. For example, if you miss out on a job at a place you liked, you could add a column for further follow-up a month or two later. You could tell the contact person that you enjoyed meeting them and that you wondered whether they had any other positions available. You would then thank them for their time and end the call.

Create a Job Search folder and have separate files for the jobs you've applied for, including your application letter, the scan of the advertisement for the job, and the position description. If the information is all together there, you can refer back to it for any follow-up you might do later.

Being organized like this will also help you with your reporting to the employment service you have been allocated to, if that's the way the system works in your country.

Plan your days around your job search rather than being ad hoc in your responses to advertisements and the approaches you might make to your connections. If you are already in work, plan the time that you have available to spend on your job search so that it has the focus it needs for you to be successful.

This is the time for me to remind you that your job search activity is not just responding to jobs that have been advertised online.

What sort of companies have the sort of role that you're interested in? Check the Jobs tab on their website on a weekly basis.

Being persistent and consistent pays off in life generally – and even more so with job seeking. Creating momentum leads to job offers.

SCAN BOTS AND OTHER HURDLES

Have you ever submitted an online job application at the close of a business day and then received a 'thanks but no thanks' email back during the night? This happened to a friend of mine and she said, 'those recruiters work very long hours!' She could have been right, but it was much more likely that her application went through a scan bot, a software program that helps recruiters sort job applications.

Scan bots will sort applications according to the needs and preferences of the employers/recruiters. Common elements that the software looks for are:

- Spelling and grammar mistakes
- Length of time in previous positions
- Length of career doing similar roles
- What school or university you attended

Your application will be rejected according to a formula that has been pre-determined. One of the most common reasons that people's resumes get rejected is that their spelling and grammar is unacceptable. In my many years of reading resumes, I have found that only about 10% of them are free from spelling and grammar mistakes.

Scan bots are becoming cheaper and soon it will not just be the bigger companies that use them. That means that more applications will go through this process, be rejected - without being seen by a warm, living, breathing human.

Why are businesses doing this? It is an expensive business to hire people and so, if they can cut out some of the time that a human is involved, businesses will save money. It means that only those applications who have passed 'the test' of the scan bot will be seen by a recruiter, employer or a human-resources professional.

Scan bots will also reject applications from people who:

- Have less than a prescribed amount of experience (and yet they could be fantastic at their job).
- Have similar skills to what is being asked for but don't have the job titles that match what has been programmed into the scan bot.
- Want to change jobs but don't have the experience.

So, unless you have submitted a mistake-free application that fits very neatly into the prescribed job with its prescribed length of experience, prescribed qualifications and went to the 'right' university, you'll probably miss out. And all of that will have been decided without your application having been seen by a human being. Frustrating, isn't it!

Of course, if all of those parametres fit with you and your career, you've got nothing to worry about.

I'm certainly not against technology but when technology makes life difficult, we have to work out ways of getting around it. If we can't do that, we have to find another way. This book presents you with a range of other ways to job search and strategies to get jobs. Stay with me if you can see that your application isn't likely to find its way through a scan bot.

OTHER HURDLES

Another hurdle I have observed is that the job seeker has a close family member or partner who is not particularly supportive of their efforts. My suggestion for this is not to engage in discussion with them about your activities and to find someone else in your circle to chat to that will be positive, helpful and constructive. Negativity will not help you with your job search, no matter who it comes from so avoid it as much as possible.

The next hurdle to talk about is the government funded service for the unemployed. In Australia, that's Centrelink. I know that it's a very frustrating system and that mistakes are often made. I suggest that you keep quite detailed notes about every interaction you have with them. Note down the name of the person you spoke with, the date, time and duration of the call, and what was said and agreed to or what actions are being taken – by them or by you. My other suggestion is to keep your cool with the staff, both in person and on the telephone. Getting a reputation for abusing the staff will not help you and may result in their non-cooperation. Being pleasant to the staff will ease your way within the system.

RECRUITMENT AGENCIES

I am not talking here of government or government-funded agencies that are supposed to provide services to people registered with Centrelink (Australian federal government agency). The following information relates to privately run recruitment services.

How recruitment agencies work

Companies looking for new staff sometimes hire recruitment services to find their new staff members. You are screened by the recruitment agency to see how well you 'fit' with the requirements of the company. The agency refers you on to the company and you may have between 2-6 interviews for the job, depending upon its complexity and level. If you get the job, the recruitment agency will be given a percentage of your new annual salary plus its perks.

The first thing you need to recognise is that recruitment agencies exist to provide a service to (mainly) big companies that are looking for professional staff. They do not exist to provide a service to you, the job seeker.

Recruitment consultants are essentially salespeople. They will source the best products (the people they decide could be the right person for the job) and make a lot of money doing that, (if they're good at what they do). They will always be looking for names of management personnel within big companies, so they can approach them to form a working relationship with them, to get their next vacancy to advertise.

As a job seeker, you will be of most interest to them if you are very skilled at your job, have good qualifications and have a sound work history with major corporations. You will also need to be professional in your approach and look professional in your grooming. They will be looking for good attention to detail, consistency and – the bottom line – how well you will fit in the organisation that is offering the job.

Given you will not know, initially, where the job role is located, it is best just to be yourself. Be honest, friendly and know your strengths. If being yourself doesn't get you past this first stage, it probably wasn't a good fit for you anyway.

The sort of person that recruitment agents find annoying are people who:

- Call them too often with no clear purpose,
- Do not have good communication skills, and,
- Are not concise in their answers to questions.

You will not get referred to the organisation if you don't listen well to the questions you are being asked and go off on tangents. You need to answer the questions that are being asked of you, concisely and confidently.

If you don't have a clear idea of what sort of role you want, don't approach them.

You may disadvantage yourself if you do this. The recruitment consultant will put your resume aside – or even delete it – if you are not focused on a specific job role. I suggest that you see a careers counsellor first to work out just what you want to do in your next role. Once you've done that, you can approach recruitment agencies with your clear intent at the ready.

If you apply for a job through a recruitment agency..

Email your application to the recruitment consultant and call as soon as you hit 'Send'. Let the recruiter know that you have just emailed your application and ask if they have received it.

Very few people do this. It's an effective strategy to make sure that your application comes to their attention.

If they answer the phone:

- Immediately acknowledge that they are busy.
- Tell them that you have applied for X job role and ask if they have received your application.
- They may do a brief phone interview on the spot. Be ready. Be positive and confident. (You may not know that they're interviewing you so don't assume their casual 'chat' is casual).
- They may say "I haven't checked yet". Be understanding and ask if there's a time you could call back to check. Make sure that you call back when you said you would.
- If they are off-hand with you, maintain your positive approach. The second that you come across as negative to them is the second they will hit 'delete' on your application.

If your goes to voicemail leave a positive, clearly articulated message for the recruitment consultant. BE RESPECTFUL.

It's OK to call in a week to see whether there's been any progress with your application but, again, remember to be polite and be ready to be interviewed again.

<u>Never</u> call to complain about anything such as not hearing from them, the way in which you've been treated, that you didn't get put forward for a job you wanted, etc. They have the power, not you. Even if you have legitimate cause to complain, suck it up and forget it.

A friend of mine was treated very badly by a recruitment consultant once and made a formal complaint to the management of the recruitment agency. She is a highly trained professional with several qualifications and the experience that almost always gets her into interviews. But she has never been considered for a position with the offending recruitment agency since. I think it's fair to say that she is on their black-list.

EVERY TIME YOU SPEAK WITH A RECRUITMENT CONSULTANT, YOU ARE BEING INTERVIEWED. However, they won't always be on your side.

A story about Christina

My friend, Christina, graduated with an Economics degree, with honours, from a top university. In her first interview with a recruitment consultant, she was told that she should give up her dream of working in corporate banking and to consider another career. Christina wasn't happy with this advice.

The second recruitment consultant she saw told her that she would be perfect in corporate banking and referred her for a position in a major bank, which she obtained. Christina continues to enjoy an excellent career in corporate banking and finance to this day.

Imagine what would have happened if she had decided that the first recruitment consultant was right. It's just as well that Christina is a gutsy and determined woman!

My point is – don't listen to people who offer you negative messages like this. That first recruitment consultant didn't really know Christina; she was offering an opinion. It wasn't based on Christina's qualification or her personal qualities of determination and tenacity.

The lesson here

If you are offered advice like this, think about who is offering it, whether they are likely to have the right expertise to make that call - and whether they have your best interests at heart.

I have heard too many stories over the years of people in positions of authority making pronouncements about young people's futures that have the potential to derail their dreams. Rather than take the approach of 'how can we make this thing happen for you?' they make dream-destroying comments that leave young people feeling shattered and lost.

Are you applying for a real job – or not?

Sometimes recruitment agencies will have a perfect candidate already lined up for a job but will advertise the position anyway. It is the only time they can legally advertise (in Australia) and means they can add potential candidates to their data base.

You won't be able to find out whether that's the case or not because any close questioning will lead to you being labelled as annoying or difficult by the recruiter. And that means that your resume will be deleted. However, if you have solid experience and qualifications in a specific field, having your resume on file at such an agency could lead to you being interviewed for another job in the future.

Again, remember that if you are called up by an agency, you must treat every interaction as if it's an interview. How you answer the phone, how confident you are, whether you can answer questions on the spot and how warm and relaxed you sound, will all contribute to you being considered a good potential candidate for the agency to put forward to their clients, the employers.

How do you know which agency to contact?

Many agencies will specialise in particular sorts of roles. An easy way to find out which agencies advertise jobs you'd be interested in is to search seek.com or careerone.com to see which agencies are advertising there and what sort of roles they have advertised.

Some agencies are quite happy for you to cold-call on the off-chance of a position in your field, others won't like it at all. So, just try it. As long as you're polite and positive, it should not go against you. Just remember that you need to be confident and direct with your answers to questions.

Specialist recruitment agencies can be sourced through a Google search. If you're looking for a job in the hospitality industry, search for specialist hospitality recruitment services in your city.

Not all recruitment agencies are ethical, but neither are some of the people who apply for jobs with them!

The bottom line

If you present as someone who looks and sounds like a professional, is trainable, is humble, respectful and motivated, you will be considered as a potential candidate by recruitment agencies.

If you present as demanding, pushy, petulant, or impatient, you won't stand a chance.

It's not about how they treat you. It's about whether you treat them positively and respectfully.

Applying for specialised roles

If you are a professional with specialised qualifications and experience, you have an extra 'ace up your sleeve' when applying for jobs.

Your knowledge of your own industry will be a great asset and you will have a fairly good idea of what businesses or organisations have the job roles for which you are very well-qualified (or have lots of experience). Create a list of those businesses or organisations, show it to someone else who works in your field and ask them whether they know of any other businesses that have similar roles.

What you want to end up with is a complete list of these businesses. Make sure that you have tagged their websites in your 'favourites' and then, on a weekly basis, check the Employment/Careers or Jobs section of their websites to see if your specific specialised role has been advertised. Some organisations don't bother to advertise on the major online job boards as they can get enough interest generated by just having advertisements on their own site.

An important next step is to systematically go through the list and note down the names of any people you know who already work for these businesses. You could then consider contacting these people to let them know that you would be interested to hear if a position became available.

Don't assume that they will feel 'used' by you taking this approach. Many companies are happy to receive recommendations and referrals for prospective staff through their current staff and offer rewards to those existing staff if their candidate is successful in obtaining the job. Some companies have a 'perks and rewards program' that provides the referrer with anything from movie tickets to a financial bonus. In this sort of company, the referrer is also likely to be publicly recognised, an incentive in itself.

Depending on your circumstances, you might also consider applying for a role that is similar to the one you're after with a view to moving sideways or up the ladder later. Some companies are hard to get into and so taking another role there can be a step in the door.

I referred to a few specialised sites in the 'Getting Smart about where to look for Jobs' section so refer back if you need to check it again. Also, take a look at 'Your Contacts – your most important resource' in the same section in case there are some connections you've forgotten.

KNOWING WHAT YOU'VE GOT TO OFFER

What skills, attributes and values do you have? And why is it important to know?

Skills and attributes are different. Skills are something you've learnt, something you can do. Operating a bobcat, cooking a meal and creating a pie-chart from an Excel spreadsheet are examples of skills.

Attributes are personal qualities you have. Examples of these are reliability, friendliness and punctuality.

Skills

As I mentioned in the Introduction, people know they have some skills, but most don't have a comprehensive idea of their skill set.

One of the problems is that when we talk about skills, many people think of the skills they have learnt at work or at college or university and they don't think about the skills that they have learnt by just living their lives. After all, you demonstrate skills every time you:

- Put on your clothes,
- Catch a bus or drive a car,
- Play a sport,
- Shop at the supermarket.

Anyway, you get the picture!

In Appendix A of this book, I have listed many different skills. You might find the information there useful in building up a list of your own skills. If you

LAND THAT JOB 73

have a particular hobby, play a particular sport or volunteer for an organisation, you will have learnt or used skills.

Think about what skills you've used and add them to your list.

To get together a list of skills that are used in the sort of job you have done previously or in the sort of job you want, I suggest that you start by writing down the skills you already know that you have. It doesn't have to be worded perfectly. At this stage you're just building your list.

Next, enter "Skills used in the XYZ industry" on Google and taking a look over what different sites come up with. You should be able to produce a list of at least 10 skills and then you can decide which ones of those you already have. (Please note that not everyone knows the difference between skills and attributes so might include 'flexibility', for example, which is an attribute rather than a skill).

The other thing you can do is look over old job descriptions you've had or at job advertisements on seek.com and see what skills are listed there.

You usually would not use (or want to use) all the skills that you have but having a master list of them allows you to copy and paste your skills onto a resume that is being tailored for a specific job.

Putting all of the skills that you have into a resume is a mistake. The recruiter or employer does not have time to read through all of them and just wants to know whether you're likely to be a good match for their job. So, handpick the skills you put on your list and make sure they're consistent with the job advertisement and the job description.

Attributes

Attributes are those qualities that you have that are specific and inherent to you. For example, being thoughtful is not something you would have learned. It's an attribute, not a skill. Similarly, having a warm personality and being able to talk easily with others are attributes rather than skills.

Employers often look for people with the 'right' attributes and some consider them more important than skills. I have had employers say to me 'I can teach someone a skill I need them to have, but I can't teach them to get along well with the other people on my team if they don't like people'.

Therefore, it is important that you put your key attributes alongside your skills on your resume. Make sure they are consistent with what the employer has asked for in the job advertisement.

Go through the list of attributes in Appendix B and highlight those you know you have. Ask someone whose opinion you value to check to see if you've missed any. It's not the time to hide your light.

Values

While you won't list your values in your resume, it is important for you to be clear about what values you hold. It can help you in determining what career you're best suited to; whether an organisation is going to be a good match for your value set; and where you want to put your energy in your life overall.

Sometimes, you might reveal your values in a job interview if your approach to your industry is similar to that stated within a company's mission or values statement.

I recommend going through the list of values in Appendix C and highlighting those that you know that you hold.

A worthwhile exercise

Often, we are blind to our own skills and attributes, especially if we are good at them. I know, it's strange but true! A really good way of discovering some of the skills and attributes that are hidden from ourselves is to do the following exercise:

Ask 6 friends or family members to tell you 6 positive skills and/or attributes that you have. Don't prompt them. Ask them to write them down for you.

Every time I ask someone to do this as a homework exercise, they come back bemused that several people wrote down something they hadn't expected. It's because that, while for you that particular skill, characteristic, or value is like breathing and therefore not something you think about, other people see that special element in you and know that it's something you do well.

Take note of these special skills, characteristics, and values because they're an important indicator of 'the thing' you have been gifted with to make your particular contribution to the world. Everyone has their own specific unique set of gifts and, if they use them in their work or business, they will experience a great deal of satisfaction – and they will make a difference in the lives of other people. (But that's another book, one I haven't written yet!)

So, why is it important to know what skills, attributes and values you have?

Firstly, it enables you to personalise your resume and ensure that it's targeted to the jobs for which you're applying. Remember that it's best to produce a resume (yourself, not through a resume service) that showcases your particular skills, attributes and experience.

Secondly, having a very clear understanding of your skills, attributes and values, allows you to see what's possible for you in a holistic way and to apply for a broader range of roles.

Next, as job roles change because of technology and other workplace changes, you will be able to identify and analyse what specific skills, etc, that you have that can then be applied to a job role that may not have even been invented yet! If you know what you have to offer, you will be able to point that out to potential employers.

If you're really clear about who you are and what you have to offer, you will have more certainty and will present yourself more confidently to the world. That will, of course, lead you to even greater success.

Take a look at the Appendices and use them to give yourself an added advantage in your job search and in your life.

> As the world we live in is so unpredictable, the ability to learn and to adapt to change is imperative, alongside creativity, problem-solving, and communication skills.
>
> ALAIN DEHAZE, BELGIAN
> BUSINESSMAN, CEO OF THE
> ADECCO GROUP

What's your online reputation like?

I have included the following excerpt from my book, *Awesome Careers for Gen Ys: easy strategies to create an amazing career and life*, just in case you have not read the book. It's really important that you take care of your online reputation because it can impact significantly on your chances of getting (and keeping) a job.

Employers often do internet checks on prospective employees. In fact, some employ people specifically to do these checks. (Now, there's a prospective job for those of you who like working with technology and are good at problem solving!)

If they see that you have made negative comments about your previous employer online, they will be concerned that you will do it if you come to work for them. Companies are always concerned about their reputations.

If they find that you get drunk or high (even if you've only done it once but there are images to prove it), they are likely to be concerned that you will not turn up fresh and ready for work on Monday morning.

You are probably thinking that you're OK because your privacy settings are fairly tight. Try putting your name followed by the words 'images' or 'photos' into Google and see what comes up. Most people are shocked to see that the photos they've been tagged in are there for all the world to see. If those photos contain some images of you drunk or high at a party, you're unlikely to get a positive call back from the employer. If you do find photos of yourself that you wouldn't want an employer to see, ask the friends who tagged you in those photos to un-tag you.

If there's a disparity between your professional presence on LinkedIn and other social media platforms, it will be noticed.

A person employed to check out your social media profile will check all of the forms of social media, not just Facebook and Instagram. Your online presence extends further than social media, of course, and so what you've said about yourself on apps, where there is a degree of public scrutiny possible (such as dating apps) is also something to consider.

> It takes 20 years to build a reputation and five minutes to ruin it. If you think about that, you'll do things differently.
>
> WARREN BUFFET, AMERICAN BUSINESS TYCOON AND PHILANTHROPIST

Is your job location important to you?

Some people LOVE working in the central business district (CBD) of whatever city they live in. They love the shopping, the nightlife after hours, the energy of being in a city. And that's all understandable.

The transport system is geared to getting people into and out of the CBD efficiently (to some extent anyway). It can be fun finding new places to eat and drink with colleagues and friends after a long day's work. There are also a lot of jobs available within the CBD. Those jobs are most likely to be advertised online and through recruitment agencies. It can be more difficult to approach these businesses directly although not impossible.

However, some people prefer to stay out of the city and avoid the peak hour traffic snarls, the daily commute, and the smog. They like the benefits of being able to be home within a shorter time frame, being able to park their car at a cheaper cost, and being able to find childcare services closer to both home and work.

So, what approach will you take to your job search if you want to be closer to home?

Check out what industrial areas and shopping centres are close to where you live. There are many jobs in both of these settings that are beyond the obvious roles you might think of.

Industrial areas are a great source of technical, administrative and sales roles. They're not just about factory workers – and factory worker roles have become much more specialised with many requiring college or university educated personnel.

It's worth checking just what businesses are operating in an industrial estate near you. Make a list of the names of the businesses there and then check them out online. What do they produce? What sort of jobs do they advertise? Going to their websites and checking the employment sections there might show you that they have a range of technical, sales, management, and administrative roles. Some of the roles may have titles that you had not thought of, but are comprised of skills that you actually do have.

As you know, shopping centres are made up of shops and employ a lot of sales assistants. But they also employ other staff as well. Think administration, cleaning, trolley collection, hospitality, and information personnel. Shopping centres may also have medical centres, travel agents, fitness centres, banks, movie theatres, and community centres attached to them. A very broad range of roles will be represented within those businesses.

Check out what businesses are located within shopping centres close to you. Obviously, big shopping centres like Chadstone in Melbourne, Australia, will have a huge range of job roles available but don't ignore your local strip shops. Within my local shops, there is a computer repair business and a pharmacy as well as the expected bakery, café, green-grocer, liquor store, and butcher. While there won't be as many jobs in the smaller shopping centres, they're still worth checking out. The added bonus is that you are very unlikely to have to pay for car parking – and you'll be able to get a park within an easy walking distance to your workplace.

. . .

I know all of this exploring of 'what's out there' takes work but that's your main task if you're looking for work – figuring out all the ways that you can get a job – and then making as many applications as possible.

CHAPTER SIX

YOUR WRITTEN APPLICATION

IT'S NOT JUST ABOUT THE RESUME!

Don't make the mistake of thinking that your resume is the only thing you need to pay attention to in the written part of your application. ALL aspects of the application will be considered by the recruiter or employer. It's critical that you demonstrate your <u>attention to detail</u> and how well you have read the information that the employer has provided about the role, the company and their requirements.

Your application may be made up of a mixture of the following:

- Your resume
- The application or cover letter
- The online application
- Responses to any pre-interview questions
- Response to the Key Selection Criteria
- The email you write when you send your application
- Any documentation the employer requests (academic records, copies of licences, etc)

THE PURPOSE OF YOUR WRITTEN APPLICATION

Many people think that they need to tell the potential employer <u>everything</u> about themselves to impress them. NO, NO, NO.

In the same way that your letter shouldn't be a repeat of your resume, your resume shouldn't include all of the things you've ever done.

The purpose of your written application is to get you to the interview.

<u>That's it!</u>

It's about convincing the employer that you want <u>their</u> job and that you have the skills, experience and attributes that make you the person they're looking for - and that you're worth the time and cost of interviewing you.

There are ways to do that effectively, and ways that will turn a prospective employer right off. Too much information is a way of turning the employer off. Including the 'right' information, targeted at the advertised job with this specific employer, gives you a much better chance of success.

What do they look for?

While you might (rightly) spend time slaving over getting your application looking good, you need to know that an employer spends an average of 5-7 seconds looking at your resume. In that time, they will be looking to see:

- Whether your overall experience is a match for the role

- Where you last worked
- If you've made any mistakes in your application
- If there are any gaps in your work history (it's fine as long as you explain them)
- Where you live (will you have to travel for 2 hours to get to us? Nooo)
- If your resume includes the keywords the employer or recruiter thinks are important for this role

If you make it to the YES or MAYBE pile, your application will be looked at more closely, but it has to make it through this critical first stage. I want you to be successful so keep reading.

The importance of having a mistake-free application

All aspects of your application need to be free of mistakes. In my experience of looking over many applications during my career, only about 10% of them were free of mistakes!

The recruiter will love these. They tell the reader that the applicant will be someone who will take the care needed when they are writing something on behalf of the company, that they will be a good representative of the company, and that they are professional in their approach.

You might be thinking, 'but I'm professional and it doesn't matter that I make a few mistakes'. Well, it does and - if you are unlucky enough to have your application read by a pedant - your application will head straight for the NO pile (or the MAYBE pile - if you've got good experience).

The employer or recruiter will assume that:

- You have poor attention to detail.
- You don't care if you make a few mistakes – so you're not likely to respect the organisation that will be paying you.
- You don't know that you've made a few mistakes – so you're ignorant.

I know that none of that might be true, but the employer only has your written application to guide them and they will take that at face value.

Your job application is a formal piece of writing

That means it mustn't contain slang or be casually written. It doesn't have to use big words or be academic (unless that's the sort of job you're applying for) but it does have to have an inherent respect within it for the organisation and for the workplace.

Formal language has the following characteristics:

- It is not personal.
- It is not conversational.
- It does not use colloquial language.
- Is written in the third person.
- Doesn't use abbreviated words.
- Avoids clichés.
- Uses the passive voice.

If you're still not sure how to write formally, Google 'examples of formal and informal writing'. The differences between the two forms will become obvious.

Be truthful

I almost didn't put this in here because I think it's obvious but lots of employers have told me about receiving applications from people that included lies about experience or qualifications. If you get to the interview stage, an employer will usually drill down and ask you questions about your experience and qualifications.

Depending on how good a liar you are, the employer may pick up on the fact that you've made something up and the interview may come to an untimely end. If you are not someone who tells lies or makes something up very often, your discomfort about this will add to your 'interview -nervousness' (it's a thing), and the employer will subconsciously pick up on it.

If they don't pick up false information during the interview, it won't take long before they figure it out when you start working for them – and then you won't be working for them! And they will be very annoyed with you. They may let other businesses know about you, too.

> Wrong is wrong, no matter who does it or who says it.
>
> MALCOLM X, HUMAN RIGHTS ACTIVIST

Be confident but not cocky

It's important to feel confident about your abilities and experience and for that to be obvious in your application. But to say that you're a 'guru' or that you are 'the best' at something will, in Australia at least, immediately put the reader off and your application may quickly find itself in the round file (the rubbish bin).

I once put an application I'd been impressed with initially into the MAYBE pile, when I read that the applicant had (according to them) 'vast experience' at something. When I took another look, I realised the applicant was twenty years' old. There was no way they could have accumulated 'vast experience' by that age, and I could see that the rest of the application was similarly littered with superlatives the applicant couldn't possibly live up to.

It's fine if you say that you have 'excellent communication skills' although it's much better if you say that you are 'excellent at delivering presentations to groups of stakeholders'. (It's much better because it's more specific and tells the employer much more than the fact that you're good at talking to people.)

You can display your confidence in yourself through the adjectives you use to describe specific skills you have. Appendix D in the back of the book lists adjectives you can use in your applications.

Some people don't feel comfortable about talking about themselves in a positive manner, so they frequently sell themselves short. They say to me, 'I don't like to boast about myself'.

It's not boasting if it's true. It's simply telling the truth about yourself.

It's important that you stop being self-deprecating. It's important for you, for your career and for the world, which misses out on what you have to offer.

Should you get your resume and cover letter done for you?

I am not a big believer in getting someone else to write your resume and cover letter for you. I think it needs to be written using your 'voice'. Paying someone to prepare your resume can result in a sterile piece of writing with no personality. They often have a generic quality about them and it's really obvious to an employer or recruiter that it isn't your own work.

I think that it's critical that your values and personality shine through and that the reader gets a good sense of YOU. (Of course, you still need to make sure that your application is written using formal language but not in a 'stiff, rod up your back' way). You will show your values and personality through the words you choose to use to describe your experiences.

If you are concerned that you will make mistakes if you write your own resume, simply ask two or three other people for help in editing or proof reading what you have written. It is worth taking some time to 'get it right'. Of course, there are many styles and formats of resumes and there is no one 'right way'. Aim to create one that you feel good about AND one where you can say to yourself 'yes, this is about ME'.

When you ask someone to help you edit and proofread your application, it is best to ask people across the generations and, if English is not your first language, asking someone whose first language is English. If you ask someone who is similar to you in age, education or ethnicity, they are more likely to make the same sort of mistakes as you. You need to ask someone with a different 'eye' to read over your application. If you do that, mistakes are more likely to be picked up and you will look better to your prospective employer.

If you do decide to pay to get a resume done for you, ask for some examples of work they've done before you part with any money. If the examples all sound the same, look somewhere else. The process should take time and the person doing it should ask a lot of questions of you either in person or through a questionnaire. They should be trying to get an understanding of who you are and what motivates you so that they can represent you well.

Consider this an investment in your future and be prepared to spend both time and money if you're working with someone who knows what they're doing.

I still think it's better if you produce your own resume and application.

THE EMAIL YOU SEND WITH YOUR APPLICATION

Your email should be brief, concise and, like the rest of your application, it should have no errors and be written formally.

All it does is to draw the attention of the reader to the attachments you've put there. The documents that you attach should be the cover letter and your resume.

If they are required, also attach your responses to the key selection criteria and copies of your qualifications or academic transcript. Don't attach these unless they are requested.

It is not a sales document unless you're applying for a sales position.

THE APPLICATION LETTER (THE COVER LETTER)

Should you have one?

There are mixed views about this but there are still plenty of people who think it's important - so you need to make sure that your application/cover letter is a darn good one.

The employer or recruiter might not read it in their initial scan of the applications that they have received (or it might be the first thing they read) but a lot of employers still want to see what sort of effort you went to in writing to them. A good application letter will reinforce the positive impression that your resume gave them. A 'one size fits all' letter will not impress them, and it could mean that your resume is not even looked at or considered. I have put applications directly into the rubbish bin if the cover letter is poorly written and littered with mistakes.

Your application/cover letter is NOT the email you send in response to the job. It is a separate document.

Who should it be addressed to?

The advertisement or the job description will tell you the name of the person who is to receive the application.

Make sure you get it right – the right spelling, the right title, the right everything!

Imagine that you're the one receiving the applications. You will come across applications where your name is spelt incorrectly or where the applicant has got your gender wrong (calling you Mr Susan Smith instead of Ms Susan Smith). How positively do you think you would view that application?

I once was on a panel interviewing for a lawyer for an organisation. It surprised me that many of the application/cover letters started off with 'Dear Sir' or 'Dear Sir/Madam' when we had provided the full name and title of our female CEO, and the applicants were asked to address their application to her. I immediately put those applications in the NO pile. I figured if their attention to detail was so poor that they couldn't do what we had specifically asked, we didn't want them in the organisation. Harsh? Maybe. But when you, as an employer or recruiter, are looking over hundreds of applications, sloppiness like this is a good enough reason to eliminate someone from the pile of applications. Attention to detail is also a fairly important characteristic for a lawyer to have!

If you know the name of the person who will receive the application, write the full name and title in the address at the top of the letter (eg, Ms Susan Smith) and then write 'Dear Ms Smith' to begin your letter. This might seem too formal, but it will come across as respectful and appropriate. If you have had a phone conversation with the person and discussed your application, it would often be appropriate to write 'Dear Susan' in the letter. You need to make your own judgement call on that depending upon the formality of your conversation with her. You still need to write her full name and title in the address at the top of the letter.

If there is no name provided for you to address your application, write The Manager or similar title and in the cover letter write 'Dear Sir/Madam'.

Even though you will be asked to address the application to one person, it will be unusual if it is only read by one person within an organisation if you are shortlisted to be interviewed. Therefore, it is important to follow the 'rules' about applying as there may be a number of people your application needs to get past before you receive a call to line up an interview.

What should the application/cover letter contain?

Firstly, it shouldn't be a shortened version of your resume. Many people make the mistake of regurgitating all of the things they've ever done and ignoring what the employer has asked for in their advertisement.

The application/cover letter needs to have enough information in there about you and your experience to peak the employer's interest - but not so much that their eyes glaze over! You need to 'cherry-pick' what you want to tell them but not tell them everything. (The exception to this is if you're a school leaver and you don't have much to tell them anyway).

Application/cover letters should not be any more than a page in length. If it is over a page, it's become too much about you and not enough about the job and the employer.

It's a bit like putting yourself forward on a dating website. In the beginning, you want to say and show enough to attract someone's interest. It's not advisable or appropriate for you to tell them everything about yourself straight away or to put a picture up there of yourself semi-clothed or naked so they see you in all your glory! In an application letter, you want the recruiter/employer to think 'this one looks like they might be a good fit for the job' – you've attracted their interest. If you tell them everything, it will be too overwhelming, and they might even find you boring.

Format

The first paragraph of your application letter (usually just one sentence) should state what job you are applying for and where it was advertised.

It should go on to say why you think you are a good fit for the job/ what skills and qualities that you have that make you an ideal candidate.

That will mean that you have researched the company, looked at their website and re-read the advertisement so that you know why you ARE a good fit with the company.

Next, it should provide some examples of roles you've filled or experiences you've had that have been referred to within the advertisement. This is important. Often people just fill up their application letters with information about themselves WITHOUT REFERRING TO WHAT THE EMPLOYER HAS STATED IS IMPORTANT TO THEM! If your letter acknowledges the employer's requirements – by referring to things mentioned in the advertisement or in the position description – the employer will immediately assume that you're in alignment with them. It will also be obvious that you are taking their advertisement seriously and that you are really interested in their job. They are key factors in getting to the interview.

I like to finish an application/cover letter with a sentence that outlines several characteristics I have that I believe the employer will appreciate. I will have chosen these from my list of possible characteristics based on my analysis of what the employer will find appealing.

I close the application/cover letter with a statement such as 'I look forward to meeting you at an interview'. I make this bold statement because I think that my application shows that I am a good fit for the job.

Again, don't re-write your resume in the application letter – provide the employer with just enough relevant information for them to want to go to your resume to learn more about you.

If you re-write your resume in the application letter it will make the letter (i) too long, and (ii) it will be focused on you rather than what the employer wants. Your letter needs to show why you are the best person for this job <u>and</u> be written with the reader in mind. The reader is the employer (or recruiter), and **they are focused on getting the right person into the job**. In a way, you come second. It is a balancing act.

Too many people forget who is reading their letter. They are so focused on getting the job that they forget to write the letter <u>for</u> the reader. They write it for themselves, about themselves, and they get the balance wrong.

Style

Job applications should usually be written in a formal style unless the job you're applying for is particularly creative or the advertisement specifically states that they are looking for someone ultra innovative and different.

Many employers expect to receive an application that is written formally. They see it as a mark of respect and that you know how to respond to the situation appropriately. A good application will demonstrate that you:

- Can write well – concisely with good grammar and spelling
- Have thought about what the employer is looking for and respond to that
- Understand the 'rules' of interacting with businesses and organisations

The reason they want this is because you will need to demonstrate these behaviours as an employee of theirs. If your application is not well written, etc, they will make the assumption that you may not be a good employee of theirs. Therefore, style is not just because someone is pedantic, (although they might be), but also because of what it says about you.

Why is it important to create a different letter for each position you apply for?

Every employer wants a person who wants their specific job. They don't want someone who is applying for lots and lots of jobs indiscriminately. Now, you might be applying for lots of jobs, and that makes sense, but your aim is to have each employer believe that their job is the one you really want.

You can only do that if you have carefully analysed their advertisement, worked out

what key qualities and qualifications they want and have written a letter that uses that information in quite a targeted way.

Your cover letter should act as an invitation for the employer to take a look at your resume, not to replace it!

It's critically important that your letter is addressed to the right person, at the right company, for the right role and has the correct date on it. You might not have done it, but way too many people cut and paste and forget to change the details on their application letters. You can guarantee that your letter will end up in the rubbish bin if you have not paid close enough attention to those details and made sure that you have it all correct. That's another reason for getting someone else to proofread your work!

It will help you to write a targeted letter if you have recorded all of your personal data in a folder. If you've done that, you will then be able to copy and paste information about yourself into your application letter and your resume.

> We are all, each and every one, unique in the Universe. And that uniqueness is what makes us valuable.
>
> JAMES A OWEN, WRITER, ILLUSTRATOR

More Useful Tips:

- Read through advertisements 3-4 times to really get a sense of what the employer wants
- Highlight the important words
- The important words are things they might say about **the company** (in this instance, they have highlighted three important factors right at the top); about **the role** (receiving orders, making sure there's no damage and that they are then correctly warehoused – *the word 'correctly' is a clue to the qualities they want*); and about **the sort of employee they want** – honest, committed, reliable, punctual, strong work ethic and with good attention to detail
- When you write your letter, you need to make sure that you use this information in a deliberate way
- Don't repeat everything back to them word for word. Repeat some of it - but use synonyms for the rest. For example, you could say that you're responsible instead of reliable.

Over the next few pages, I have included a couple of advertisements and written targeted application letters that demonstrate a careful analysis of the advertisement. See if you can pick out what I have done.

Advertisement no 1

Warehouse Store Person / Picker Packer – Croydon

Fast growing online retailer
Family-owned business
Small team with great company culture

The company is an online retailer of quality products available for delivery Australia wide. We are a small team but growing fast. In line with that growth we require a full time store person / pick packer to join our warehouse team.

You will be required to have a high attention to detail in all aspects of your work. It is important that you are able to work both as a team member and autonomously, taking responsibility for your work in a fast paced environment. You must be honest, committed, reliable and punctual with a strong work ethic. Previous experience in a similar warehouse environment preferred but not essential.

Your day-to-day duties and responsibilities will include:

Picking & packing of orders. Assist with the receiving of deliveries and unloading of trucks. Ensuring that all products are received as ordered, undamaged and correctly warehoused.

Sample application letter for position in Advertisement no 1

The Manager (when the advertisement doesn't have a name for you to respond to)
X Company
Address
Email address

Date

Your address
Your mobile/cell number

Dear Sir/Madam (use this format when you DON'T know who is receiving this letter)

I am writing to apply for the position of Warehouse Store Person/ Picker Packer that was advertised in The Age on 25th February 2020. My resume is attached.

As a reliable, responsible person with good attention to detail, I think that I am an excellent candidate for your position. When I was a student, I worked part-time in the Stores area of my local Target store and so have experience in receiving stock and both warehousing it or distributing it promptly to the correct department.

In my current role as Team Leader at Kentucky Fried Chicken, I have a responsibility for stock control and frequently have to receive goods from our transport company. I ensure that these products are quickly stored in accordance with food handling regulations. In this role I have a team of six staff reporting to me. Staff morale is high, and we enjoy working together.

I take pride in the work that I do and enjoy working as part of a team to get a job done well. I am also happy to work independently on tasks. I am excited by the prospect of working in a dynamic environment such as X Company and would welcome the opportunity to be part of a positive, growing business.

I look forward to meeting you in an interview.

Yours faithfully   (use 'faithfully' when you DON'T know the name of the person you're writing to)

Your name

Advertisement no 2

Social Media Manager

We are seeking a Social Media Manager to join our team.

The Social Media Manager will implement the company's Social Media Marketing. Administration includes content strategy, develop brand awareness, generate inbound traffic and cultivate leads and sales. The Social Media manager is a highly motivated individual with experience and a passion for designing and implementing the Company's content strategy, creating relevant content, blogging, website construction, and leadership.

Executial Duties:

Manage Social Media marketing campaigns and day-to-day activities including:
Curate relevant content to reach the company's customers.
Create, curate and manage all published content (images, video and written).
Monitor, listen and respond to users in a "Social" way while cultivating leads and sales.
Conduct online advocacy and open stream for cross-promotions.
Develop and expand community and/or blogger outreach efforts.
Oversee design (ie: Facebook Timeline cover, profile pic, thumbnails, ads, landing pages, Twitter profile, and blog).
Design, create and manage promotions and Social ad campaigns.
Design, create and manage multiple webpage designs.

Compile report for management showing results.
Marketing company products via all media types.
Demonstrate ability to map out marketing strategy and then drive that strategy.
Become an advocate for the Company in Social Media spaces, engaging in dialogues and answering questions where appropriate.
Executing creative social media campaigns.

Qualifications and Experience:

Possesses knowledge and experience in the fields of marketing.
You must demonstrate creativity and a passion for Social Media, with in-depth knowledge and understanding of platforms including Google+, Facebook, Twitter, Instagram etc. and how each platform can be deployed in different scenarios.
Makes evident good technical understanding and can pick up new tools quickly.
Possesses outstanding communication skills.
Extensive experience in webpage design is required.

Please forward any questions and applications to: admin@xxxxxxx.com.au

Sample application letter for position in Advertisement no 2

Jenny Zhang
Director of Communications
X Company
Company address

Date

Your address
Your mobile/cell number

Dear Ms Zhang   (write her name formally like this)

I am writing to apply for the position of Social Media Manager that was advertised on Seek on 6th March 2015.

You will see from my resume, attached, that I graduated with Honours in Marketing in 2017. Since then, I have been employed in ICT marketing roles in a contract position at Wizz Banger and in my current role at XYZ Plus. I am highly motivated and keen to be considered for this role.

I relished the challenge, at Wizz Banger, to design and create approximately 45 websites that were focused on increasing the profit possibilities for clients through the use of the various social media platforms.

In my current role at XYZ Plus, I have honed my skills in marketing campaigns across the major social media platforms. Charged with the task of developing brand awareness of the company on social media and to foster this approach within the company itself, I have been actively involved in assisting staff in the use of Twitter and in using blogs to communicate their particular expertise and knowledge. I have also further developed my ability in determining and driving social media marketing strategies while at XYZ Plus.

My passion for using social media as a key marketing tool plus my technical expertise across ICT makes me an ideal candidate for the position of Social Media Manager with your company. You will find that I am a positive and dynamic communicator (in both writing and in person) who will bring creativity, attention to detail, the ability to learn and generate new ideas quickly, and an attitude of responsibility mixed with good humour.

I look forward to meeting you at an interview.

Yours sincerely   (use 'sincerely' when you know the name of the person you're writing to)

Your Name

YOUR RESUME

Your resume is your primary sales document. It must be as good as you can get it so that it sells YOU well.

It may be distasteful for you to read those words but that is the reality. Having a resume that is poorly written, has mistakes, and doesn't give the employer or recruiter a sense of who you are (and why you are the person they should hire), sells you short. You won't get to the next stage of the process if your resume is crap. It has to showcase YOU! Get comfortable with that idea. It's important.

Having said that, you need to know that an employer faced with reading a pile of resumes for a position they've advertised, may only look at the top half of the first page of your resume before deciding whether to read on or whether to put it in the No pile. So, while it's a big mistake to have spelling or grammatical errors within your resume, it's particularly important that the front page is perfect.

It's also important to customise your applications so you may need to tweak your resume for each job to which you apply. More on that under How many Resumes should You Have?

Format

There are a lot of sample resumes online that you can use. Chose a format that you feel comfortable with but don't chose something that is all flashy formatting, fonts and graphics. That's especially important if you don't have a lot of actual information to put in there. More on the content of the resume shortly.

A problem with having highly creative formats, fonts and graphics is that the scan bots (the software that reads and sorts job applications) has a hard time coping with them and often rejects them before it has been seen by a human being.

I always emphasise the need to make your resumes as simple and concise as possible, while also using the keywords of your industry.

Whitespace

You also need to chunk your information, have headings and dot points, and ensure that there is plenty of whitespace on the pages. It is <u>MUCH</u> better to have three pages of a resume with plenty of whitespace than two pages of crammed information for the employer to read.

An acquaintance of mine once asked me to look at his resume. It was jam packed with information, had hardly any whitespace and had complex formatting. I told him that he needed to make it much simpler, have more whitespace, and take it from the two pages he'd used to three pages. He refused and was unemployed for a long time.

Having more whitespace on resumes is not just a personal preference of mine. It's because it will make your resume easier to read and understand. A study by Dmitry Fadeyev from Wichita State University (one of many on the topic), found that 'properly using whitespace…can increase comprehension up to 20%'.

This is what you want! If your resume is easier to read and understand, it has a much better chance of making it to the 'Yes, we'll interview' or 'Maybe we'll interview' piles. The employer or recruiter will actually pick up on the information you're providing much more easily when a resume is well written and has plenty of whitespace.

WHAT TO INCLUDE IN YOUR RESUME:

Your contact details

This is self-explanatory, but you need to make sure that the employer or recruiter can reach you to arrange an interview. Double check that your contact number is written correctly.

Make sure that your email address is professional. If your regular one is something like sexychick69@gmail.com, please create a new one that is plain and ordinary for your job applications. It is small things like this that can make the difference between being interviewed – or not.

As well, if you have a voicemail answering service activated on the number you have on your resume, make sure that it is appropriate for an employer or recruiter to hear.

Your skills and attributes

It's important to know your key skills and attributes so that you can write them here but it's also necessary for you to be clear about them for the interview. I have already referred you to Appendices A and B to help you with this. Limit yourself to a combined list of skills and attributes of about 8-10 items.

It's important that you make sure that the list includes at least some of the attributes that are asked for in the advertisement for the job. Use the word or a synonym for it.

A Roget's Thesaurus is a useful tool for finding alternative words to the ones the employer has used in the advertisement. Finding an alternative word is sometimes better than just repeating what they have asked for in the advertisement.

Your employment history

This must be listed with the most recent first then work back from there.

A common error that people make is to highlight/put in bold the name of the company they worked for rather than the position that they held. Employers want to check out your career progression or to see how you have expanded your knowledge and experience with different roles. They also want to check out how stable your work history is and so won't be impressed with a long list of jobs where you only stayed for a few months. One job of that length is OK but not most of them.

There has been a significant movement towards a preference for achievement-based information under each job role and a significant move away from providing a description of the duties you undertook during your time at the company. Employers want to be able to see what a difference you made while you were with that company, what you brought to the role that made you a good employee. More on this a little further down.

This is the case even if you were working in a casual role as a waitress, for example. In that case, you could talk about how you cheerfully welcomed every customer into the business within the first two minutes of their arrival or that you never made a mistake with a customer's order.

If you have been working in a higher-level professional role, it's important that you write down about three-four significant achievements for each position. The achievements should be quantifiable and use the language of the role. For example, you could write that as events manager of the hotel, you increased the number of events held in the corporate business rooms by 15% during your tenure.

Where you can use percentages or numbers, do so. The employer wants to know that you can make things happen. It will back up your claims of being dynamic or energetic or results-driven.

The employer will gain a more comprehensive understanding of your skill set and that you have a good level of self-awareness and an understanding of what's important in the business world.

Writing down a list of duties doesn't tell an employer all that much. They will not have any idea of whether you performed those tasks well, expertly or half-heartedly. Some people have found this a difficult concept to move on from so I usually set them the task of writing one sentence that describes the main duties they undertook and then going on to write their three major achievements in the role.

How far back do you go?

Your work history should really only go back for the last 8-10 years. I suggest that you would then make a list of positions prior to that time with just the position titles and the company names. Don't add in the dates.

There is some ageism by recruiters and employers that will work against older workers. If you have a long work history, I suggest that you format your resume quite differently and instead of a chronological history, list the roles you have had under one heading and companies you've worked for under another. You could list your key achievements or awards you've received under a different heading again, although you would be best to link specific achievements to the relevant company. You might want to start with your most recent role and call that My Most Recent Role (or whatever you want to call it).

This is also a good strategy if you have had a stellar career in a field yet don't want to continue working at that level. Older workers are often keen just to continue to make a contribution to their industry rather than seek a higher-level position. Being too specific about their experience can give the prospective employer the wrong message. They may think that you want to continue to work in a higher-level position and that you're just applying for their role to get your foot in the door.

Gaps in your employment history

There will be many people who will have this issue as a result of Covid19.

There are two things you must do.

1. Explain the gap (even if it's obvious),
2. Provide some details of what you did during that time.

I wrote about this in The Most Commonly Asked Questions section but will repeat a few things here as a reminder.

If you re-organised your garage, painted your house, created a veggie patch, or worked on a small renovation of your home, include that in your resume to show the employer that you didn't spend the shutdowns of the pandemic on the couch, watching Netflix and drinking wine. I also suggest that you list out the achievements related to your activities.

If you volunteered somewhere or helped out people in your immediate neighbourhood, include that too. Friends of mine sewed masks, some for charity and some as a small business.

Employers will be pleased to read that you took initiative, that you are someone who looks for things to do, and that you are an active participant in life.

Some of you might have a gap in your employment history because you have been parenting or caregiving for a few years. That's fine but make sure NOT just to say that BUT to add in the skills you used while you were doing that. You can also list your achievements from those years in the same way that you would list them for a paid position.

Don't make the mistake of minimizing the role you had and think that you didn't learn or demonstrate any skills during that time. As a mother and a caregiver, I know that I have learnt a lot from those roles. Use your favourite search engine to identify the skills involved in each of the tasks you performed and add them to your resume.

If you have been a volunteer, that work can be added into the Employment History section of your resume if you were not working in paid employment at the time you were doing it. It will then explain any gaps in your employment history. Obviously, you would include your achievements from that role as well.

Education/Qualifications/Training

This heading will depend upon the position to which you're applying.

Generally, if you have some employment experience, I suggest that this section is put after your employment history. The exceptions to this are if you are a school leaver OR if the application advertisement has focussed on your educational level as a central requirement of getting the job.

As with your employment history, your most recently obtained qualification is written first and the second most recent is written second, etc. That is, it needs to be written in reverse chronological order.

If you have formal qualifications, TAFE (community college) and in-house training, you put the formal qualifications first followed by the TAFE (community college) qualifications and then the in-house training after that.

Volunteer work

If you have volunteered out of work hours, create a separate heading for it and provide information about the organisation you volunteered for, the role(s) you took on and the period of time you worked for them. If it is a regular annual program such as The Smith Family Christmas Hampers, write something like '2009 – current' if you expect to continue doing that role.

Achievements

These need to be quantified rather than generalised. A figure (sometimes a dollar figure) needs to be included in your list of achievements under the roles you've had.

An example could read 'Wrote 9 articles on business start-ups and technology, generating 88,010 page views, 7,937 page likes, and 2,715 tweets'.

Just saying that you wrote articles for your company's social media platforms is inadequate but quantifying it like this gives it more impact.

If you can't think of things you've achieved, ask a friend, colleague or mentor. If you're a school leaver, write in anything you were involved in at school, such as the State Mathematics Competition or that you were on the SRC (School Representative Council). Also, write in how long you held that position.

If everything you have done is as part of a team, say something like 'I was a key member of a three-person team that....' Alternatively, you could mention the role that you specifically played in the team. For example, if you were the person who always checked the numbers, you could state 'the team relied on me to check the accuracy and validity of the figures in the project' and then go on to specify what the project did in more detail.

Awards

These could be listed under your achievements related to your employment, but I think they have more impact if they're written under a separate heading.

You also need to provide sufficient information about the award. What does 'Won Swinburne TAFE's Tradesperson of the Year' tell you? Not much. Writing something like 'Won Swinburne TAFE's Tradesperson of the Year Competition: 2018 (9 trade areas, 250 applicants, 10 shortlisted).

Write the full details of any acronym you use in your description. Make sure that the recruiter knows how special the award is and what competition you faced. I have rarely seen people do this section well. It's as if they're embarrassed to say that they've been recognised for being good at something. Stop that thinking right now! Remember that it's not boasting if it's true plus if it gives you an edge, use it.

Interests

Please don't write 'watching television'. Employers don't want couch potatoes. They want people who do stuff.

I always like to see what people write in this area to see how interesting they are, and it can provide me with a starting point to a conversation. It gives you a chance to start building a relationship with the employer or recruiter.

If you write Passionate Demons Supporter, it gives them a chance to talk football with you. If you write Avid Reader of Autobiographies, it gives your interviewer a chance to ask about which ones you've read or who's inspired you. Those responses are a whole lot more interesting than just writing Sport or

Reading and make you more interesting to the employer.

Referees

Some people don't like to include these until they're being interviewed, and that's OK.

If you do include specific names and contact details, make sure you do the following:

- Check the spelling of their names and email addresses
- Include their position so that the employer knows that they were above you in the pecking order.
- If they are no longer at the company, say so on your resume.
- Triple check that you have written their mobile numbers correctly. (You would be surprised how many times I have called a referee only to find the number was incorrect).

When you have some experience in a field and you are applying for another position in that field, it is a good idea to include a referee who is respected in that field. I once interviewed someone whose application wasn't all that great but who had listed a referee who I respected enormously. It can get you through the door of the interviewing room.

Obviously, you cannot write in the names of parents or relatives. My sister once called a referee for someone she was looking at hiring and, during the course of the referee check, it became obvious that the referee was the partner of the woman who'd applied for the job. Naturally, that ended the applicant's chances of getting that job.

What not to include in your resume:

- Your date of birth – unless it's your first job and the position is for a junior or requires a 'school leaver'.
- Your marital status and whether you have children – in Australia it is illegal for the interviewer to ask about those things.
- Your state of health (unless it's something specified in the advertisement).
- A Career Objective – it's passé to have a career objective and puts the focus on what you want rather than on your suitability for the position you're applying for. It is sometimes appropriate to have a short (not more than two sentences) Career Summary at the beginning of the resume.

How many resumes should you have?

If you have several areas of interest and/or expertise, create a separate resume for each of them. Generally, you would have somewhere between one and three resumes. For example, if you have a couple of major areas in your degree such as 'marketing' and 'ICT', you could do a resume that focuses on marketing and one that focuses on ICT. You would not ignore the other part of your studies or experience, but you would make sure that you place more emphasis on your marketing information ahead of ICT or vice versa depending on the position you were applying for.

Each of the resumes would highlight any experience you have within a particular field and the skills you list would have particular relevance to that specific field. It's about bringing the experience, skills and interest that you have in a particular field to the forefront. The reader needs to see that the resume has a particular focus.

Make it obvious to the employer (or HR person reading the resume) that you should be considered because you have some of the experience or skills they're looking for in their candidates.

Changing occupational fields & changing your resume

Sometimes people come to me and say that they want to change fields altogether but are not sure what to do or how to present themselves to a new 'market'.

The first step is to analyse what skills are inherent in the 'old' job. Go online and Google it. Make a really comprehensive list of the skills and then use a highlighter to determine what skills you actually enjoyed using in the 'old' job. If you still want to keep using those skills – and they probably are what you still want to use - include them on the new version of your resume.

The next step is to work out what job roles might use those particular skills. If you know what roles you'd like to apply for, analyse what skills are used in those jobs and see if there is anything in common from your past positions.

Some occupations have quite distinct ways of presenting information. Schools, for example, often has quite prescriptive formats for teacher applications and it can take a fair bit of work to change that to something that is commercially appropriate. It's worth the trouble, though, because teaching gives people a huge range of transferrable skills. They just need to be teased out and then presented in a very different format. If you know someone who has made that sort of transition, talk to them about the changes they had to make to their resume.

Go online again and find resumes suited to the sort of role that you'd like to get into. See if there is any jargon or specific phrases or words that are common across the resumes and make sure that you incorporate them into your resume.

If you don't know what roles you'd like to do, then I suggest that you (i) read my book *Awesome Careers for Gen Ys: easy strategies to create an amazing career and life*, or (ii) talk to a good career counsellor.

Consider creating a YouTube clip

Think about producing a short video of yourself (2 minutes is fine, 10 minutes is way too long), within which you talk about yourself, your skills and your values. Download it to YouTube. You can put this on your website and put a link to it on your resume.

This is really a group task because, to get the best result, you need others' opinions of what you've done. It does need to be professional and appropriate. Be dressed professionally. Don't have the video shot with you in your favourite hoodie or ten-year-old T-shirt.

You need to make sure that it doesn't work against you through an amateurish effort. Just be yourself. Don't try the hard sell unless that is genuinely who you are.

SAMPLE RESUMES

The following pages have a couple of sample resumes. As I have already mentioned, there are many formats and versions of resumes. Look online to see which ones appeal to you personally.

Brad Jones   This resume is from a school leaver looking for a retail job.
12 Station St
Danyo
03 8888 9999
0444 444 444

Skills & Characteristics

Establishes rapport easily with people of all ages and ethnicities
Loves being part of a team
Willing to learn
Enthusiastic and positive
Reliable and punctual
Good literacy and numeracy

Education

Completed year 11 at Danyo College   2018

School Involvement

Class Captain   2017
Member of the School Representative Council   2015-17

Sport

Member of the Eastern Hornets Basketball Team   2015-
current

Hobbies

Keeping fit (running)
Writing a blog for the Eastern Hornets Basketball Team
Family activities

Referees

Jenny Mack   Rob McIntyre
English Coordinator   Year Level Coordinator
Danyo College   Danyo College
03 8888 1171   03 8888 1171

RESUME

Doula Liolios
45 Mackie Close
Danyo
03 8888 6666
0444 414 414

Skills and Characteristics

- Excellent website design and implementation skills
- Dynamic communicator (both in writing and in person)
- Positive attitude
- Very sound knowledge of social media platforms, their uses and possibilities
- Ability to produce workable, creative marketing strategy plans
- Broad range of technical skills in ICT
- Ability to learn and adapt quickly to change
- Responsible and reliable

Employment History

Social Media Marketing Officer   2016-current
XYZ Plus

Responsible for:
- Implementing the company's social media marketing strategy; driving the expansion of social media use across the company and with our clients; and designing and creating promotions, campaigns and webpages

Achievements:
- Increased the use of social media by staff by 350% in a two year period
- Developed a targeted, detailed social media strategy plan to replace general statement of intent
- Revenue from social marketing campaigns has produced $1.2m in sales over 2 years

Website Designer in Marketing Department (contract position)   2015
Wizz Banger

Responsible for:
- Designing and creating 45 websites with specific requirement that the sites maximised the use of social media platforms

Achievements:
- Completed the project on time and on budget
- Received very positive feedback about all websites with minimal changes being requested

Education and Training

Level 1 Occupational Health & Safety Certificate — 2017
Conducted in-house at XYZ Plus

Bach of Business (Marketing) (Hons) — 2014
Banksia University
Majors in Marketing & ICT

Community Involvement/Sport

Coach for the Under 13s Eastern Wanderers Girls' Soccer Club — 2012-current
Member of the Eastern Wanderers Women's Soccer Club, B Division — 2010-current

Hobbies

Running (have completed 2 half-marathons)
Gym
Water skiing

Referees

Bill Lee
Head of Marketing
XYZ Plus
0411 111 111

Tiffany Bell
ICT Manager
Wizz Banger
0412 111 111

A FEW TIPS ABOUT RESPONDING TO KEY SELECTION CRITERIA (KSC)

This is a part of the job application that I have seen handled badly too frequently. Applicants often see it as an opportunity to write about their philosophy about their role or career rather than an opportunity to provide evidence of having used that skill or demonstrated the capacity to handle a situation in the past.

The evidence can come from a range of sources. Obviously, if you have employment experience, you select your evidence from that, in the first instance. I also suggest providing evidence from at least two different jobs as that will show that you have used that skill in more than one setting. If it's appropriate, you can also select evidence from your non-work life, too. For example, if one of the KSC is Leadership, you could also include having been on a board of directors or having coached the local basketball team.

- Don't do it as part of your letter (unless the employer specifically asks for you to do that).
- Write your response as a separate document entitled 'Response to Key Selection Criteria'. In your heading, write the name and number of the job as well as the name of the company. Create a footer on the right-hand side with your name on the first line and, on the second line, write 'Applicant for… the name of the job'. This is to set up a subtle link of your name with the job itself, in the mind of the recruiter.
- Don't give them your philosophy about life

or your occupational field in your response. **This is NOT a document about your beliefs.** It is a document that sets out how you have demonstrated particular requirements of the position in previous roles (including work, leisure, volunteering, sports, etc). It's providing evidence that you have used that skill before or have the specific qualification or licence that they've asked for.

- Use dot points and make your information succinct and focussed. (It can make the reader's eyes glaze over if they are presented with a block of text. Break it up.)
- I use a maximum of four dot points under each criterion. I also show how I have used that skill or demonstrated that quality in different roles that I have had. (That way the prospective employer can see that this is something you have consistently done throughout your career. If you are new to the workforce just keep that in mind for next time you apply for a position.)
- Provide concrete examples of your experiences for each of the selection criteria. These examples should demonstrate how you did something AND, ideally, quantify your experience. See examples on the next page.
- Please note that it doesn't have to be complicated. What you're demonstrating is your ability to use a specific set of skills NOT providing an essay about yourself and your philosophy of life.
- **Use the STAR technique to come up with your answers. S = situation**

(where were you); T = task (what task/job/problem had to be solved); A = activity (what did you do to solve the issue); R = result (quantify the outcome/ show what you achieved)
- By the way, this STAR technique is one that is useful in job interviews to describe how you dealt with a particular problem. It helps keep you to the point and has your answer be succinct.

Some examples of responding to key selection criteria follow.

Sample Responses to Key Selection Criteria

Criterion 1: Demonstrated excellent communication and interpersonal skills

- For the six-monthly review of our department in July 2019, my peers and I presented a workshop to the whole of the staff at Jill Johnston Pty Ltd that was aimed at informing staff about our key project. I was selected as Master of Ceremonies and received positive feedback about my performance from the General Manager.
- I achieved a trophy for Best Evaluation Speech in my Toastmaster club's annual speech-craft event in 2018
- As a Year 12 student at Danyo College, I was runner-up in the college's speech competition in 2016

Criterion 2: Ability to plan and implement events and activities

- I initiated, planned and led the implementation of the inaugural Student Cooking Boot Camp at Banskia University in 2015
- I assisted my aunt on a stall at the Mildura Festival in 2016 by creating flyers for the event, posting about it on social media, delivering products for the event and then staffing the staff with her for the day
- As a Year 12 student at Danyo College, I was one of four students who planned and implemented our Year 12 Formal Dance in 2017

With both of these examples I have tried to show how someone might have developed an existing skill or tendency for something over time. Employers will be able to see that you have built on a skill they're looking for and could reasonably expect that you will develop it further while you're employed by them.

This is also why it's a really good idea to record everything you do in a separate folder. We do forget things we've done and yet they can be very useful ways of demonstrating a skill we have.

Sample Responses to Key Selection Criteria

Criterion 1: Demonstrated excellent communication and interpersonal skills

- For the six-monthly review of our department in July 2014, my peers and I presented a workshop to the whole of the staff at Jill Johnson Pty Ltd that was aimed at informing staff about our key project. I was selected as Master of Ceremonies and received positive feedback about my performance from the General Manager.
- I achieved a trophy for Best Evaluation Speech in my Toastmaster club's annual speech-craft event in 2012
- As a Year 12 student at Danyo College, I was runner-up in the college's speech competition in 2010

Criterion 2: Ability to plan and implement events and activities

- I initiated, planned and led the implementation of the inaugural Student Cooking Boot Camp at Banskia University in 2014
- I assisted my aunt on a stall at the Mildura Festival in 2013 by creating flyers for the event, posting about it on social media, delivering products for the event and then staffing the staff with her for the day
- As a Year 12 student at Danyo College, I was one of four students who planned and implemented our Year 12 Formal Dance in 2012

With both of these examples I have tried to show how someone might have developed an existing skill or tendency for something over time. Employers will be able to see that you have built on a skill they're looking for and could reasonably expect that you will develop it further while you're employed by them.

CHAPTER SEVEN

APPLYING ONLINE

ONLINE RESUMES/VIDEOS

If you are applying for a role where your ICT skills are a key element of the role, or where you want to feature some online events, programs or apps you've produced (for example), it makes sense to create an online resume. It has to be professional, polished and attractive to the viewer.

You would cover elements of a written resume but not necessarily in as much detail. You would include links to your productions, and you would feature as the narrator.

I suggest that the video itself not go longer than about five minutes, but the linked material could be longer.

ONLINE APPLICATIONS

Some organisations ask all applicants to submit their applications via an online form. There are some general principles that you need to follow:

- Make sure that your resume is up-to-date and easily accessible to you. You will invariably be asked to attach it to the online application.
- Have referee details handy as, even though they may be on your resume, you may have to list them separately.
- Some companies will not have a 'save and return' option so make sure you have all of the things you might need at hand at the time. Allow enough time to complete the form.
- Look over the company's website before you start. It will refresh your memory about their values, locations, products or philanthropic endeavours. It may provide you with ideas for your answers.
- They may expect you to provide examples of how you have handled difficult situations or provide other scenarios for you to comment upon. Re-read the scenarios section of this book to remind yourself about how to answer those questions.

CHAPTER EIGHT

THE INTERVIEW

INTERVIEWS

Interviews don't just happen in a recruiter's office or at a business. Sometimes you will be asked to participate in a telephone interview, either live or automated; or to respond to interview questions by videoing your responses to questions provided by the business or recruitment firm and then submitting them to the recruiter or company.

Increasingly, we are being asked to attend interviews through an online Zoom meeting (or similar). Some companies ask people to attend group interviews as the first step in the recruitment process; and some of those ask participants to work as part of a team to complete an experiential task.

Similar principles apply across all interviews so in the first section of this part of the book I will deal with the interview that happens in a recruiter's office or at a business. At the end of this part of the book, I will provide some specific tips for the other types of interviewers.

You can do this!

Remember that I said that you can learn the skills of both the written and interview stages of the job application process. Let's assume now that you've mastered the skills necessary to get you to the interview stage.

Even if you are someone who is not naturally a 'performer' or someone who has a lot of self-confidence, you can still be successful if you plan ahead and practice what you're going to do and say during the interview.

You will not have made it to the interview stage if you hadn't already shown that you have at least some of the skills and qualifications the employer is looking for in their next employee.

So, what is the purpose of the interview?

You might think that the employer is looking for someone that has the right skills and qualifications for the job and then offer it to them. However, <u>many studies show that employers are more concerned about your personal characteristics AND how well you will fit into their team</u>. Your resume and cover letter has told them that you have something of what they're looking for. Now they want to see what you're like – in person!

The employer will be looking for personal qualities such as likability, integrity, courage, self-understanding (including knowing your strengths), problem-solving, love of learning, responsibility and working well in a team. You don't have to be extroverted to be able to demonstrate those things.

You do need to be able to convey that you have them – and you can learn to do that AND still be yourself.

Sometimes the purpose of the first interview is to weed out who they don't want so that the rest of the interview process can be focussed on the two or three candidates that the employer thinks is most suitable for both the role and the company. Second and third interviews will be focussed on determining how you think and act in specific situations, whether your values are aligned with theirs, and whether you really are the person you said you were in your written application.

Of course, most employers will only conduct one interview for their vacant position and so you will need to demonstrate – in that one interview - that you have the personal characteristics that they are looking for plus whether you can problem solve, think analytically, communicate effectively and whatever else they think is important for the role. If you've already held a job or several of them, they will probably have a reasonable idea of what skills you have.

Skills identification is something that most people aren't good at – and that's why you need to be able to say what skills you have, both in writing and verbally. Appendix A, all about Skills, can help you with that.

An Interrogation or a Positive Exchange: What's your view about interviews?

A lot of people get nervous about job interviews because they think that they are at the mercy of the interviewers and that it's about whether the interviewers like them or not.

Job interviews are actually about both parties working out whether they're a good fit for each other. The best interviews are truly interactive with both parties asking questions and gaining an overall sense of what the other party is like.

Essentially, the employer wants to find out whether you would fit in with the existing team and whether you have the qualities they think are important in getting the job done well. They will know from your written application that you have at least some of the qualifications, skills and attributes they want, but they want to delve further to see if you're likely to get along with the other staff and what sort of attitude you will bring to their company.

Ideally, you should be there to see whether this is the sort of place you want to work. You're there to check out whether this is an environment where you are able to use your favourite skills with people who are good to work with, in a role that will be satisfying to you because of your own needs within the employment context.

I know that not all interviewers are good at what they do. I once walked out of an interview because the employer kept taking phone calls rather than actually conducting a respectful interview. I figured that if he were that disrespectful when I was a prospective employer, he'd be even worse if I got the job. Because being respected is a key value of mine, I knew it wasn't going to be a good match.

Some interviewers are nervous and uptight because interviewing is not their field of expertise. Believe it or not, you can help get the interview onto a positive footing by being relaxed, smiling and maintaining good eye contact. If you engage with the interviewer with a quiet confidence, they are likely to respond back in the same way.

> You've got to understand – when you're interviewing someone, it's not an interrogation. It's not the Nuremberg Trials.
>
> JOAN RIVERS, COMEDIAN

Preparation

The key to performing well in an interview is in the preparation you do in the days <u>before</u> the interview. Planning ahead and practice are critical factors in having a successful interview. That means that you will need to spend time getting ready for the interview and there are various aspects to this which I'll cover in the pages ahead.

It's a big mistake to 'wing it' and live in the hope that the interviewer will be 'nice', won't ask too many hard questions and that they'll think you're just fabulous based on your charm and good looks.

If you spend a few hours in preparation for the interview, which itself might only take 30-45 minutes, you will go into the interview with the quiet confidence that will have you being considered for the role.

First things first

When you are contacted about the interview, make sure you find out the following:

- Find out specifically where you have to go for the interview, what department or site,
- Who to ask for (write the name down – don't depend on your memory, you're likely to be nervous),
- Whether you need to bring anything with you to the interview (academic records, licences, etc).

If you forget any of this, get back in contact with them and ask again. You can always say something like "I'm just calling to check on where I need to come, etc". It's better to get the facts right than going to the wrong address or department; better to know who to ask for than forgetting their name; or forgetting to take copies of your qualifications than arriving empty handed. They won't think that you're an idiot because you're calling back. You're just demonstrating that you're thorough and that you're keen to be considered for the job.

Next, work out how you're getting there and how long it will take (allowing for traffic holdups).

Will you go by train? If so, do you have the timetable? Is there anything on the public transport website about replacement buses or track work? If so, allow extra time.

If you're going by car, will it be easy to find a parking space? Will you have to have money or your credit/debit card for the parking metre? How far away from the interview site will you have to park?

How long will it take you to walk from the car to the interview site?

If you know the name of the interviewer, check them out on LinkedIn. If you're a visual person, it will also help you remember who they are at the interview because their photo will be there. What has their career been like? Do they have any particular skills or interests in common with you?

Now the practicalities are dealt with, the preparation begins in earnest!

Research

Before the interview, research the organisation by spending quality time on their website, making notes and writing down any questions that you might want to ask in the interview. Read about all of their activities from their products to their vision statement; read about their staff and their backgrounds; see how the company started and if they do any philanthropic work; and note how easy (or not) it is to navigate around the site.

See if there are any reviews or articles about the company by simply putting the company name down in a Google search. Make sure that you have a good overview of the company and its operations prior to going for the interview.

After you've spent an hour or more researching the company online, re-read the advertisement and the job description. I know you've already read it several times during the written part of the process but reading it again at this stage is useful. You will have a better idea of why they framed their advertisement the way that they did and have a deeper understanding of what sort of person they're likely to employ.

What will they ask me during the interview? OMG! I just freeze at this point!

If that's your concern, relax! I mean it. If you feel nervous at any time in the lead-up to the interview or just before the interview, take several deep belly breaths and exhale gradually. You can slow down your heart rate and breathe deeper. It's a simple physiological activity but it has a huge impact on your body. If you do this, you will put yourself in a more relaxed state and you will perform better.

It's really important to think about the questions you'll be asked in the interview, have answers already worked out AND practice saying them out loud. Get a friend or family member to ask the questions as if they are conducting the interview.

Make a list of the questions you've already thought of and give them to a friend or family member to ask you. Ask them not to critique you as you go along so that you can get into the flow of the interview.

> You might feel a bit silly and self-conscious about doing practice interviews but your performance in the interview itself will really be enhanced if you make the effort to do this.
>
> SHARON DAVEY, AUTHOR, CAREERS COACH

Commonly asked questions

There are, in fact, a number of commonly asked questions in interviews so preparation <u>can</u> be done ahead of time. <u>Always</u> have answers ready for the following, commonly asked questions:

- Tell me about yourself
- Why did you apply for this job?
- Why do you want to leave your current job/ why did you leave your last job?
- Why should we give you this job?
- What are your strengths?
- What are your weaknesses?
- Tell me how you handled a difficult situation.
- Where do you see yourself in 5 years' time?

If you have answers ready for these, you will relax a bit more and handle the interview better overall.

It's likely that you will be asked about your Covid19 experience, so I have included some suggestions about that, too.

Let's take them one at a time:

Tell me about yourself

They are not asking about where you were born or what your hobbies are. What they are wanting is:

- A brief or potted summary of your workforce experience (especially experience that is relevant to the role you're applying for). That experience can also be derived from volunteer work that you've performed

or even from a hobby you're passionate about.
- What strengths you displayed while you were doing those roles

When you answer this question, you'll also be letting them know what your confidence level is like, how personable you are, whether you can sum things up well and how self-aware you are.

Your response to this question can set the tone for the interview so if you practice your answer and feel very comfortable in your delivery of it, you will boost your confidence for the rest of the interview. Your comfort level will be felt by the interviewers and they will, in turn, be more comfortable and relaxed.

Don't practice until your answer sounds rehearsed. It should still sound natural – down-to-earth and confident.

It's important to keep your answer to a manageable time so I suggest that you practice a response that is around 1.5-2 minutes in length. It will be longer if it's a professional role but still generally no more than 3 minutes.

Why did you apply for this job?

The focus here should be on you moving forward and how you think you can contribute positively to the organisation. Again, you can indicate a strength or two you have that you know they're looking for (because it was in the job advertisement).

Do not talk in a negative way (in answer to this question or ANY other) about your previous position or boss – unless you don't actually want the job. Any negativity will be interpreted in a negative way. Bad mouthing a previous job or employer is a huge NO/NO. If that was your reality, you will need to work out how to re-frame it.

So, your answer to this question needs to focus on how, in this potential role, you will be able to learn, grow, gain more/deeper experiences, do more than you've been able to previously, etc. You will be able to use specific skills (which you would name) to add to the company's productivity, enhance their reputation, make them more successful in the marketplace. You will need to be able to provide more concrete examples of how you will do these things, depending on your experience and the role you're applying for. I hope my words have given you a sense of how the answer needs to land with the interviewer. You're looking forward and their company is where you want to work.

While you may talk about building on skills you've gained in the past, it has to focus on aspects of the job or company that make it a more attractive proposition to you than those you've faced previously. It will be on things such as their niche or their breadth, their size (bigger or smaller) and how that suits you better, the sort of products they make or services they offer, or even their great philanthropic program.

Essentially, you need to show them that you're excited by this particular position and keen to get it.

Why do you want to leave your current job?

Studies show that most people leave jobs because of the following factors:

- Poor leadership – most people move on because of problems with their boss,
- They didn't have room to grow or learn,
- Wanting a better work culture,
- Wanting more challenging work.

All but one of these reasons is perfectly OK to give as an answer if you are asked this question. You have probably figured out that the answer <u>you must not give</u> is that you had a poor manager or supervisor. Speaking badly about a former boss has you look unprofessional. A recruiter might wonder how you will handle it if you get another boss that you don't get along with and may not want to risk putting you forward for jobs. Again, you must not talk negatively about a previous job or employer. You're the one who loses if you do that.

You might also need to be careful about saying you want a better work culture in case there is a tinge of negativity in your tone. It would be best expressed by saying that you'd heard great things about their work culture.

It would also be fine to say that you want to work more locally (if the role is a lot closer to home).

The recruiter/employer will know that this could be a difficult question to answer and part of what they will be assessing is the <u>way</u> in which you answer it. Are you being confident or evasive, positive or negative, down-to-earth or hesitant? Your attitude to life, and your ability to handle difficult situations, will become apparent both from the words you use and the tone in which you say it.

Being prepared, really prepared, to answer tough questions with confidence will work very much in your favour so spend the time to prepare well.

Why should we give you this job?

This is where the rubber meets the road and your preparation for the interview can really pay off.

What the employer wants to know is what your strengths are, why you think you are a good fit for the role and the organisation.

It's important that your response shows how YOU are an excellent candidate and does mean that this is not the time to go all shy and bashful. This is why you MUST know, and be able to articulate, what your strengths are and what you will bring to the company. That's also why you need to have re-read the advertisement and position description so that you're clear about what they want.

If you've got a written list of your key skills (and I hope you've worked out that it's essential to have done that) and you've practised being able to articulate them, your answer will be 'on target'. Tie these skills to your experience for these answers and you will have nailed it.

You might find it useful to draw up a table, have a column for each of your skills and another column for the experience where you used that skill, so that you can see how you can tie them together. Use this table in your practice interviews and you'll see the difference being well prepared can make.

I've attached lists of skills, attributes and values in Appendices A, B and C at the back of the book. Check through them to help you identify your own lists.

I've had people say to me that they don't want to boast about themselves during a job interview but boasting is very different from stating facts.

If you've got the experience, if you've got the skills, if you have the attributes they are looking for – tell them. It won't be boasting unless you say it using a boastful tone of voice. It will simply be you giving the interviewer information. If you don't tell them, who will? They won't be automatically calling your referees, not at this stage. You can't even assume that they've read your resume thoroughly, so you need to tell them who you are and what you've got to offer them. If that's hard for you, it means you need to practice even more.

This is one of the answers where naturally quiet and shy people need to practice that little bit harder. You CAN learn how to speak positively about yourself. It might just take a little more time and effort for you rather than for your more outspoken peers, but I know you can do this. I've helped people practice talking about themselves positively and seen great improvements.

What are your strengths?

This really is the same question as the one above. Answer as I've suggested there. If they ask you both questions, just be more specific in this one.

This question gives you an opportunity to talk about your inherent characteristics such as honesty, trustworthiness, and your ability to easily get along with others. As well, you could mention your record of punctuality, of getting tasks done within deadlines or about having good attention to detail. Obviously, you need to be honest about this and it should be easy to find examples in your life of where you have demonstrated these things.

This question could also give you a chance to talk about specific technical and professional skills you have that relate to the role you're applying for.

Again, it's not boasting if it's true. Just watch the tone of your voice when you're telling them about what you're good at so that it lands like a simple statement of fact rather than 'get out of my way, I'm freakin' fantastic'. If you're worried about it, just practice a bit more.

There is further information on communicating your strengths in the More Ways to Improve your Performance during your Interviews later in the book.

What are your weaknesses?

The reason for this question is for the employer to find out if you have some level of self-awareness and whether you will take the opportunity to grow or not.

There was a time when coaches told applicants to turn their weaknesses into strengths and say things like 'I'm too much of a perfectionist and will stay back to make sure that I deliver a great result'. Interviewers are not silly and know that this was a tactic that was once recommended, so this is an approach that I do not recommend.

What works is being honest. If the prospective job involves occasionally delivering presentations and you don't like public speaking, you should say something like "I don't really feel comfortable with public speaking" <u>AND</u> then say what you are doing or intend to do about it. So, you could say "..but I have joined Toastmasters to become more comfortable as a public speaker" or "..but I intend to enroll in some public speaking classes at my local college". Obviously, what you say must be true.

The principle here is to:

(i) state your weakness (preferably something in a peripheral aspect of the job you're applying for), and then,

(ii) say what you're doing or going to do about it.

The employer will see that you're a person who is honest, has a level of self-awareness and who is willing to grow and develop their skills. Win/win.

Tell me how you handled a difficult situation.

This is a very commonly asked question and the employer genuinely wants to know what sort of approach you'll take. There's not necessarily a 'right' answer to this question but it will show the employer how you think and how you solve problems.

Give a concrete example of a situation that actually happened. (Have a couple of examples ready). If you have employment experience, choose something from a job you've had; and if you are new to the workforce, describe something from school, college, a volunteer role or even from your social life. Be specific and outline how you handled the situation.

The employer wants to know how you would react in a difficult situation in <u>their</u> workplace so you need to be able to say what you learned from the situation and how you would handle it more effectively next time. That will also show them that you have a capacity for reflection and self-awareness.

This one can be tough if you haven't thought it through so brainstorm with family or friends to make sure that you come up with a sound answer. Again, practice your answer.

A version of this question is often put into hypothetical scenarios. I'll talk about them shortly.

Where do you see yourself in 5 years' time?

This question is less commonly asked these days but may still be asked by an 'old-fashioned' or inexperienced interviewer so it's best to have an answer ready.

What employers are wanting to know is how committed you are likely to be to the company, whether your career aspirations are a fit with the role you're applying for, whether you set goals, and whether you have the potential for growth and promotion. They also want to know if you know if you're going to stay. It costs money to train a staff member and for a new employee's productivity to build up so they don't want you to leave too quickly.

Clearly your answer to the 'where do you see yourself…' question should not be anything like "to be CEO" if you're applying for an entry-level job. But it should demonstrate some sense of the skills that you would like to develop in the role. It might include how you would like to learn enough about a department to be considered for a supervisory role in that area, for example.

You could mention that you're interested in doing further study in something related to the role or related to management, and then tie that to the position for which you're applying. This has to be true, of course.

Covid19 related questions

The other question which is likely to be asked immediately after, and probably up to several years after, the pandemic is over will be something like 'what did you do during Covid19?' or 'what did Covid19 teach you?' or 'how did Covid19 change you (or your life)?'

You will have acknowledged any gaps in your employment for this time in your resume but talking about your experience will also tell the employer what sort of person you are, whether you have compassion, initiative and common sense. What is your general approach to life? Are you a positive or negative person? Are you practical, kind, part of your community, or a rebel? Your answers will reveal a lot about you.

Obviously, saying something like, "well, I spent a lot of time on the couch watching Netflix and drinking beer/wine" is not the way to go! That's not going to impress a prospective employer.

Nor is it a good idea for you to start talking about conspiracy theories or say, 'it was only old people who died anyway'. You don't know what life has been like for the person sitting across the desk from you. They may have lost a dearly-loved grandmother or may have suffered mental health issues as a result of Covid19 and a flippant or thoughtless answer will not do you any favours.

The question is your opportunity to show how you approach life. Did you start a veggie garden, clean out all of your cupboards, re-organise your garage, get fitter and healthier, do a lot of walking, join neighbourhood groups on Facebook or Snapchat, contribute to others, read a lot of books, enjoy spending time with your family? All of those things are fine to talk about.

If you undertook some sort of project at home, no matter how banal or small it might seem to you, tell the interviewer what you did. You can prepare for this question by thinking about what it was you did, working out what skills you used to do it, and what you learnt while doing the project, whether it was about yourself or the task at hand.

If some of you were able to contribute to others in some way, talk about what you did. If you walked an elderly neighbour's dog or mowed their lawn, tell the interviewer. You won't be bragging; you'll be showing them that you are thoughtful and caring.

Some of you may have taken the opportunity to create a small business. I had a couple of friends who made masks and then advertised this on their local area Facebook group. One went to a local trendy shop and asked whether she was interested in selling them and the owner said yes. An interviewer will see this as you having initiative.

Another converted their front yard into a thriving vegie patch and sold the produce to his neighbours. He has been able to talk to interviewers about planning their patch, how they went about it, what they learnt and how it was satisfying to themselves and their neighbours.

One of my friends joined the board of directors of a small charity. She has been able to demonstrate to prospective employers that she is a responsible person and a contributor in their field through taking on a leadership role in a voluntary capacity.

There are many examples I could give you about how people used their time during Covid19 that demonstrated initiative, diligence, compassion, leadership, community spirit, good organisational and time management skills and entrepreneurship. Think about what you did during Covid19 and how you can provide examples of your positive attributes and skills.

The bottom line is that, if you haven't worked out and practised your answers to these commonly asked questions, you will have done yourself a disservice. It could be the difference between getting the job – or not!

Hypothetical Scenarios

If you're applying for a position where you would be expected to have a reasonable level of knowledge and expertise already, you may be asked questions in the form of scenarios. Scenario questions are more sophisticated and are often not handled well. Therefore, I suggest that you spend some time working on answers to scenarios that you dream up yourself. That will really give you an edge and could be the difference between you getting the role or not.

Firstly, think about what situations might commonly occur within the role and how you would handle them. They will usually be related to difficult or tricky situations that commonly occur in your industry/field. Scenarios are likely to be based around issues such as:

- Handling difficult people,
- What you would do in a situation of conflicting priorities,
- Your actions or responsibilities in an emergency,
- How you respond under pressure,
- Testing your knowledge about who the client actually is (eg, parent, child, school, government department).

If you get asked about some hypothetical situations, you're more likely to do well if you've already thought about possible scenarios. Write down about 4-5 scenarios and, for each or them, make list of:

- The stakeholders who would be impacted in some way by the scenario (they might include the organisation, its customers, its staff, its board of directors)
- Who has responsibility in the situation? (That might be several people, departments, agencies)
- What decisions have to be made?
- What possible courses of action could be taken?
- What will your role be in responding to the situation?

If you consider all of these aspects of a hypothetical situation, you will provide a thorough answer.

Most people answer scenario questions inadequately because they haven't thought through the elements of the scenario.

They tend to focus on just what <u>they</u> would do, and they don't think more broadly about what others will need to do, who needs to be communicated with, what the impact will be to the organisation or one or more of the other stakeholders. Their answers often show that they don't automatically see themselves as part of a team.

If you have friends and family who are willing to help, ask them to provide input into the aspects of the hypotheticals and then ask them to use the situations to conduct a mock interview with you. (People tell me that it's way scarier to be interviewed by friends than by the actual interview panel!)

When you are working out the different elements and possible answers to scenarios, you are likely to get different answers and suggestions from each of your friends. That's fine. There are no real right and wrong answers to scenario questions and recognising that will help you come up with a better answer.

I promise you

I promise you that you will feel more relaxed and will handle the interview better if you have done the groundwork and have practised your prepared answers beforehand.

If you want to watch some videos on interviews, I have included links to my YouTube channel in Appendix F of this book. I have a number of 3-4 minute videos on YouTube about interviews and job search.

On the day of the interview

One of the biggest mistakes that you can make – and that employers hate – is to be late to the interview.

So, allow plenty of time to get dressed and groomed.

Take a copy of your application with you, the whole enchilada. Have it in a neat folder.

Allow plenty of time to get to the site of the interview. I am a bit anal about this sort of thing and tend to get to the place I need to be at least half an hour early. I find a coffee shop and have a coffee while I do a last-minute read through of the job advertisement (yes, again) and the position description. I also read through my application letter. I get myself completely into the 'head space' for this role. (After all, it is not the only job I've applied for, so I don't want to get mixed up with the applications I've made).

Then, take yourself to the site of your interview, making sure that you arrive where you need to be 5-10 minutes early.

Be pleasant to the person behind the reception desk. That person is usually the one person in the organisation who knows who everyone is, and their opinion is often valued. The boss or supervisor may ask them later what you were like when you arrived, whether you were easy to speak to and whether you were well-mannered. If you were rude, off-hand and didn't engage with them, they will tell your interviewers anyway!

I think the single most important thing for a job interview is leave the phone in your bag and do not look at it for 20 minutes (or for however long the interview lasts).

JOANNA COLES, EDITOR, USA

IN THE INTERVIEW ITSELF

Entering the room

When you enter the room, shake hands with all the interviewers. Make sure that you shake firmly and don't leave the interviewers with the feeling that they've just had a limp fish land in their hand. Repeat the names as they say them. "Nice to meet you, Jane". If you don't catch their name, ask for it to be repeated. I don't have a good memory for names, so I try to remember at least two of the panel members' names.

If you're new to the workforce, don't be alarmed if you find there is more than one person conducting the interview. It is quite common for interview panels to consist of up to three people. Less common is having a panel of four or five but it can happen.

Be conscious that everything that you say and do provides an employer with information about you. I once interviewed someone for a role and almost terminated it before we began because he brought in six full supermarket bags to the interview room. He obviously hadn't thought about how this would be perceived by me, the interviewer. If he had asked the receptionist whether she would take care of them while he was in the interview, it would have created a better impression.

Seemingly innocent questions may be ways for the employer to determine what sort of person you are and what sort of attitude you have. Questions like 'did you find a parking space easily?' or 'have you enjoyed the weather we've been having?' are designed to elicit a response that tells the employer how you approach life. It's a good idea to frame any responses in a positive way.

Responding to questions

If you're not sure how you're going to answer a question, repeat it slowly to give yourself time to come up with an answer.

If you're not sure if you were on track with your answer, ask your interviewers if you got off track and if there's anything else that they want to know in relation to that question.

If you don't understand the question, say so. Ask them to repeat it or say 'I didn't understand about…' Your honesty and confidence in asking will be seen a lot more positively than if you try to bluff your way through – that won't work!

If you've prepared for the interview you will be more confident and less stressed. Knowing how you will respond to some of the questions you'll be asked will ensure that you're more relaxed than if you had gone in completely unprepared.

Don't forget to smile!

You might forget to do this in your nervous state, but it is really important on a number of levels.

One, the employer will see you as someone who is easy to get along with and will think you have a positive outlook. Two, the impact <u>on you</u> of smiling is significant – even if you're faking it!

The movements of muscles in your face (during the act of smiling) trigger endorphins that are released into your body. Endorphins are responsible for making us happy – and they lower stress levels and lower blood pressure. So, even if your smile is a polite one rather than because you actually feel happy, you will get some of that feeling anyway. Endorphins help reduce the stress hormone cortisol, so it actually causes us to feel more positive.

If you remember to smile in the interview, you will be helping yourself relax and feel more comfortable.

At the end of the interview

After the interviewer(s) have finished asking their questions, they will usually ask if you have any questions. Always try to have something you can ask about. A question or two about induction or training is the way to go. Ask about what your induction will include or about whether they run any in-house training.

If it's a medium or large organisation, you could also ask if they have a buddy or mentor person.

If they have asked you where you see yourself in five years, answer the question and then ask, "do you mind me asking where you would see this position leading to in the next five years?" This will help you see what the employer is looking for and whether they've thought ahead as well. This is part of you being an active participant in the interview so don't shy away from these sorts of questions.

If you have noticed on their website that they engage in philanthropic activities, you could ask them about that program, how it works, how their staff are involved in it, etc.

Ask them when they will make a decision about the job and when you will be notified.

DON'T ask about what you'll be paid or when you can take holidays. Those things can be discussed when they call you to offer you the job. At that stage, you know that they want you and your negotiating power is much stronger.

If you are a bit unsure of how you've come across, feel as if you didn't perform well or just want to reinforce your commitment to the job application, let the interviewers know at the end of the interview that you are really keen to be considered for the role. As an interviewer, I have been impressed when applicants have said that to me. It shows me that they're not just going through the motions and they are genuine about their application.

Thank your interviewers at the end of the time and shake hands with them all again, making sure you look them in the eye as you do so.

After the interview

A post-interview thank you is a great way to stand out from the rest of the applicants. Sending an email, thanking them for the opportunity to meet with them, is a noteworthy action. Sending or dropping in a hand-written note of thanks is an excellent way of being seen as a keen applicant.

If you have not heard from the employer within the time they specified, call and ask whether a decision is likely to be made soon. Don't assume that they have made a decision and haven't called. Workplaces are busy. Sometimes, hearing back from referees involves a fair bit of 'phone tag' and may not get completed within the period that was specified at the interview.

Always thank them afterwards, regardless of the decision they have made. Leaving them with a good impression of you can pay off at a later date.

Getting good feedback about your interview performance

You can seek feedback either at the time that you find out that you didn't get the job, OR do it later.

If you have been unsuccessful, **NEVER ask 'why didn't I get the job?'** The employer will immediately become defensive or cautious. They will be fairly closed about their answers and you won't get any useful information for next time. They will be responding to the potential emotion within that statement and be concerned that you could erupt in anger.

ALWAYS ask 'what can I do next time to improve my performance in an interview?' Asking for assistance is much more likely to elicit a positive and constructive response than asking a question that could have the interviewer feeling defensive. Most people like to help when asked. Really listen if they provide you with constructive feedback. It's not always easy to hear but can turn out to be quite useful to you for future interviews.

If you are getting interviews and you are not successful, it's time to seek some feedback.

Call up the lead person for each of your interviews for the past two weeks, tell them that you are getting a few job interviews and not getting any job offers. Let them know that you are conducting a review of your interview performances and ask whether they could let you know how you could improve your performance next time. You need to approach them using a neutral tone with no hint of anger, recrimination or victimhood in your voice.

This approach will sound less emotional and you will come across as someone who is just being analytical about their situation. The interviewer is more likely to open up and provide you with useful information.

If the interviewer is relaxed and open with you, ask them questions like:

- "Were my answers to questions on target?"
- "Were my responses thorough enough?"
- "Did I talk too much?"
- "Was my physical presentation appropriate?" Or "Did I wear appropriate clothing to the interview?"

If you sense that you have an area of weakness, create a non-emotional question around that area and include that in your review.

Getting a NO

If you hear from the employer and their answer is 'no thanks' and you would have really liked that job, send them a thank you for letting you know and let them know that you would still be interested in the role if their chosen applicant doesn't work out for them.

Otherwise, you just need to accept that the position was not for you – and move on. Continue with your job search. As I have previously mentioned, you need to have a number of applications in the pipeline at any one time, applications you're writing, applications you've sent and other interviews to attend. You also need to have lists of people to contact and follow up on. This application should have been just one of a number of actions you've been taking to get employment.

Being in action, and staying in action, will be what gets you a job.

OTHER FORMS OF INTERVIEWS

Group Interviews

Group interviews are sometimes held if:

- The employer is looking for more than one person,
- Teamwork is a significant component of the role and they want to see how you perform as part of a team,
- To establish who the leaders will be in the team,
- To see how you solve problems as part of a team,
- To see who in the group has initiative, observes well, is prepared to speak up with different ideas, etc.

The group may be asked an ethical question or a question that is confronting to see how you handle that in a group. If you can handle the questions well, it will be surmised that you will be able to deal with a stressful or fast-paced environment on the job.

Questions might include:

- General interview questions (have a 20 second response ready to the commonly asked questions I spoke about earlier).
- Case studies (speak up and say what you think)
- Practical tasks (contribute, be involved)
- Role-playing exercises (just relax and go with it)
- Group presentations (the employer will be looking to see how you worked as a team, how you solved the problems you were presented with, and who took the roles involved, such as leader, researcher, organizer, etc).

General principles if you want to perform well in a group interview:

- Be prepared,
- Be yourself (the relaxed version)
- Be confident, and
- Be a good listener.

If you are a leader, allow that aspect of yourself to shine. This is not the time to be a wallflower.

These types of interviews usually favour the extraverts amongst us but keep in mind that employers also want people who listen well to instructions as well as working well together. They will be observing how positively you interact with others, whether you smile at others, and whether you contribute to discussions or not. You don't have to be loud and 'out there' to do those things.

INTERVIEWS USING TECHNOLOGY

Telephone: Live

Covid19 restrictions have led to more of the 'first step' interviews being conducted by telephone. It's harder to have an interview without the visual cues we usually have so the following tips could help:

- Relax and smile. A smile comes through in your voice.
- Have all of your notes and written responses to the commonly asked questions beside you.
- Make sure that external noise is minimised so that you can hear each other easily.
- Project your voice well and don't mumble. They won't have any visual cues, so your voice needs to be clear.
- Have your application, their advertisement and paper & pen beside you.

Telephone: Automated

These sorts of interviews are usually time-tabled, and you will be expected to call at a certain time. You will have to provide answers to an automated voice and will have to answer around 5-10 questions for a set period of time (eg, 3 minutes) for each question.

It is likely that your answers will be converted to text and fed through a scan bot to determine whether they want to talk with you further. That is, you will be sorted in or out through software rather than a person. You will only get to the next stage – where a real person is involved – if you have been able to handle the automated process well.

Given your words are likely to be converted to text verbatim, all of your ums and ahs, hesitations and stumbling will be converted as well. If there is too much of that, you may not get to the next step. How's that for pressure! And you wondered why I was spending so much time talking about reducing anxiety!

Video Interviews

These are different from Zoom meetings or similar technology. Here I am talking about interviews where you are provided with the questions ahead of time and then asked to record your responses on video. Again, your responses may be put through a scan bot and converted to text, etc, but the recruiter/employer is getting a lot more information about you than just your verbal responses.

I suggest that you consider the following:

- Have bullet-point notes for yourself for each question to serve as a reminder for the things you wish to cover in each question. Have them in a neat pile beside you.
- The background is clean and uncluttered.
- The lighting and sound are good.
- Smile and be as relaxed as you can be.
- Dress professionally.

Make sure that you submit the video within the time provided.

Zoom/Online Interviews

During Covid19, many of us became very familiar with Zoom meetings, even if it was just a drinks party with friends. Most of us saw how other people lived or, at least, appeared to live.

More Zoom/online job interviews are being conducted post-Covid19 to be able to quickly sort out job applicants. The time and cost of interviewing people in person is considerable and employers are looking for ways to minimise that cost.

I know from personal experience that there can be a world of difference between the written application and the way someone presents in person. Employers have told me that there are added layers of complexity when it comes to online interviews.

Obviously, if you are given a time for an interview, <u>you must log on at the time you are given</u>. If you don't have the courtesy and time management skills to do that, forget about being seriously considered for the job. Punctuality is a key attribute that all employers look for in an applicant. If you want the job, you'll log on at the right time.

Imagine that you're an employer talking to a prospective employee in a Zoom meeting and you notice any one of the following in the background:

- A bong on the person's benchtop
- Unmade bed
- The house/apartment in an absolute shambles
- Evidence that the house/apartment is filthy
- Lots of unwashed dishes or clothing
- Other people wandering around (sometimes in a state of undress)

These things may be acceptable to you and your friends but is not likely to impress a prospective employer. The employer is unlikely to say 'yes, sure, you've got the job'. They are likely to be completely turned off by what they will see as your laziness, your questionable habits, and the fact that you couldn't get your act together to present yourself as a professional?

So, your background needs to:

- Be clean and uncluttered.
- Have no clothing in piles, pet bowls and litter trays, dirty dishes in the sink, etc.
- Not have other people wandering through (it wouldn't happen in the office so it shouldn't here either).
- Good lighting and sound (do a practice run-through beforehand with a friend if you'd like to check).

You need to be dressed as you normally would for a job interview, either smart casual or in business attire.

Have notes but not lots of paper. Clutter sends a message that you're not organized. It has to appear as if you have it all under control!

CHAPTER NINE

MORE WAYS TO IMPROVE YOUR PERFORMANCE DURING YOUR INTERVIEWS

USING YOUR VOICE WELL

Keep your chin up and project that voice forward.

That doesn't mean yelling. It means don't mumble or talk so softly that the interviewer has to strain to hear you. If they can't hear you or understand what you're saying, they will think that you're 'hard work' and you will not get any further in the process.

Using your voice well is facilitated by good breathing, breathing down into your lungs rather than taking shallow breaths into the top of your chest. Taking deeper breaths will also help steady your nerves and help you come across as more confident.

If we don't feel confident, we are more likely to mumble or not project our voices well.

This is something that is relatively easy to improve. It just takes practice.

Practice projecting your voice forward:

- When you're in the shower

- Driving somewhere or stuck in traffic
- Taking a walk
- Talking with friends

Becoming used to projecting your voice forward, and focusing on breathing well, will be enormously helpful in job interviews.

HOW YOUR LEVEL OF CONFIDENCE IMPACTS YOUR PERFORMANCE IN INTERVIEWS

People feel a lack of confidence for many reasons:

1. They believe that they don't perform well at interviews. Don't make it become a self-fulfilling prophesy.
2. They view the interviewer as being in control of the interview and as the person with all the power. A change of perspective, and an understanding that this is an interactive conversation where you are checking each other out, is needed.
3. They are desperate for a job because they have no money (see below).
4. They don't have much experience.
5. They are concerned that they will say the wrong thing.
6. They are taking it personally.
7. They actually don't have the skills that are needed and are scared the interviewer will find out.

If you go into an interview under-prepared and feeling uncertain, your breathing will be shallow and your overall demeanour will suggest to the interviewer that there may be a problem with you. They may interpret that as:

- you are actually incompetent and trying to hide it, or
- you don't have confidence in your own abilities, or
- you're distracted by something else and not focused on the task at hand (ie, being interviewed for a job).

A hesitant and nervous manner could lead the employer to decide that you are not the right person for their job before you've even opened your mouth!

Belly breaths are your friend. Use them to steady yourself and you will appear and be more confident.

COMMUNICATING YOUR STRENGTHS

As I've already said, one of the key things to do to increase your confidence in job interviews is to know your strengths.

Some clients have told me that they feel as if they can't say what they are good at because that would be 'boasting'. There are three things that I usually say to that:

- If it's true, it's not boasting. It's simply stating facts.
- If you don't or can't say what you're good at, the employer/interviewer won't find out. They're not mind readers.
- The job will go to someone who <u>can</u> and <u>does</u> articulate their strengths.

HOW you communicate what your strengths are will make a difference. For example, if you say, 'I'm the best bricklayer in Australia by far and no one can match me', that's boasting and is not likely to win you any jobs.

If you say, "I am a good bricklayer because I make very few errors and have little wastage", that's stating facts. Your tone of voice and the words you use are important. If you say something like "I suppose I'm OK at bricklaying" it will suggest to the employer that you have very little confidence in your abilities and they're unlikely to employ you.

Practice stating what you're good at in a firm tone, with your chin up and a smile on your face.

If you're not sure what you're good at, there are plenty of sites on the internet that can help you identify your skills and personal characteristics. To help you get a start with this, I have added three appendices at the back of the book that can help you get started. Do the exercises there and firm up your understanding of what you've got to offer.

If you have a particular area of expertise, Google 'skills needed to do X (area of expertise)' and see what things you can add to your list of strengths. You are not likely to be good at all areas within your field so make sure that you can identify and speak about those that are your strengths.

Don't be too general in creating your list of skills. I have seen 'good communication skills' written in so many resumes that it no longer has any credibility to me. If you isolate out the specific communication skills that you are good at, it will be much more effective. Reading about someone's ability to write detailed, thorough and concise reports, for example, gives me a much deeper understanding of the sort of person they are.

Communication is about speaking, writing and listening. What specific skills do you have in those areas?

Please note that communication skills and interpersonal skills are different and ensure that you have specific examples to show how you are good at both of them, if you are asked.

An exercise I ask my career counselling clients to do is to ask six people they know (people who are positive about you) to write down six skills or characteristics that they believe that you have. Not everyone will say the same things, but it will give you a start in creating your lists. If several people say the same things about you, and that often happens, make sure that you include those skills and attributes in your job application documents and interviews.

FEELING DESPERATE ABOUT THE JOB INTERVIEW BECAUSE YOU NEED THE MONEY.

I've been in this position and I know that you have to work just a bit harder with your interview preparation to minimise the impact your anxiety will have on the interview.

Make sure that you have created a list of possible interview questions pertinent to the role and practised your answers; practice your answers to the most commonly asked questions; determine what clothes you're going to wear and make sure they're clean and ironed; and read and re-read the advertisement and job description so that you're really clear about what they want. That's all the 'bread and butter' stuff.

Work hard on bringing down your level of anxiety. It's possible to do that. It's not just important to do so, it's critical to your job search success.

REDUCING YOUR LEVEL OF ANXIETY

Meditation

If you meditate, do that. Do it more frequently than usual. Do it on the train on the way to the interview or in the car once you've got to the interview site.

If you don't currently meditate, start. There are plenty of studies that demonstrate that meditation reduces anxiety. There is plenty of information online to help you get started and you don't need to pay for any courses to learn. There are many videos on YouTube and soundtracks of meditation music, all for free, that can get you started.

Breathing

Breathe. Deeply, right down into the bottom of your lungs so that your belly sticks out. Let it go gradually. Do it four or five times, counting to four breathing in, hold for a count of two, breathing out to a count of four.

Again, YouTube is a source of videos on how to do this.

Breathing deeply once you get to the interview location can really reduce your anxiety level. Do about four deep belly breaths and you will find that you are less anxious.

Reach out to a positive connection of yours

Call someone who really believes in you and ask them to tell you why they think you'd be great for this job.

If you did the exercise at the top of the page that suggested you ask your friends to tell you about your skills, read those over to remind yourself that those people think well of you. Your breathing will probably slow down, and you will become more relaxed as a result.

Get inspired

Take a CD of an inspirational speaker and play that in the car on the way to the interview. Or read a chapter or two of an inspirational book, once you get to the site of the interview.

Visualisation

While some of you might think this is a bit woo-woo, there are plenty of studies from reputable universities that show that imagery and visualisation works to improve performance. Athletes have been using it for years and now it is being used in other fields, as well.

It has become a well-known fact that we stimulate the same regions of the brain when we visualise an action and when we actually perform that same action. Athletes visualise themselves running and winning races, imagining themselves feeling confident, confident, and successful with plenty of energy left. And it works!

So, use it for your job interviews. Imagine walking into the interview room feeling happy and relaxed. See or feel yourself interacting well with the interviewers, answering their questions with ease. Focus on your feelings and feel yourself being confident, comfortable, calm, positive, and relaxed. Practice that in your mind, over and over. When you get to the real interview room, flick your mind to the visualisation you created in your head and evoke those positive feelings.

IF YOU SEND OUT LOTS OF APPLICATIONS (SAY 10+) AND DON'T GET AN INTERVIEW, STOP.

It's time to review.

I know that the market is especially competitive right now so it means that you will need to pay close attention to every step in the whole job search. Sending out lots of written applications and not getting an interview means that it's time to review your job search strategies:

- Review the content, wording and format of your application letter and resume. Read this entire book. Ask people you know (who are experienced at writing or reading job applications) for feedback.
- Review where you're looking for jobs. Are you just applying online? Big mistake right there.
- Are you using a broad range of sources to look for work from online applications through recruitment sites, individual company sites, government websites, LinkedIn, etc?
- Are you using your contacts in the comprehensive way that I've discussed in this book? Remember that about 80% of successful job applications come from our contacts and networks.

IF YOU GET LOTS OF INTERVIEWS AND DON'T GET A JOB, STOP.

It's time to review.

Not getting a job after having been interviewed a few times means reviewing what you're doing at the interview.

So, I suggest that you review:

- Your preparation for the interview. Take on board the need to practice, practice, practice. Ask the most positive members of your family and friends for assistance and to act as mock interviewers for you.
- The interview itself. What part of the interviewing process lets you down? Work on that. If you don't know, call someone who interviewed and ask for feedback. (More on that below).
- Practice meditating or listening to inspirational podcasts if you get very anxious at interviews. Practice breathing deeply so that you can reduce your anxiety very quickly when it's needed.
- Write down any questions that you've been asked in an interview, work out how you will answer them if you're asked again and practice your answers.
- Practice answering the most commonly asked questions, over and over. That WILL reduce your anxiety and you will perform better.
- Think about your post-interview strategies. Do you send through a thank you to the interviewer? Do you ask for feedback on your performance?

- Your referees. Are you certain that you have the right telephone number for them? Do you send them a copy of the job description prior to going for the interview so they have time to look at it and consider your suitability to the role? Are you really confident that they will say positive things about you? Sometimes they don't and, if your gut tells you that's a possibility, work out who else can be a referee for you.
- Are the contact details for your referees current and up-to-date? As an interviewer, I have been surprised and disappointed by the number of times that I have called to do a referee check and found that the number was incorrect or not connected. I usually called the applicant back to get a current number, but it reduced my confidence in them, the applicant. Sometimes I didn't bother, and the job went to someone else.

OTHER REVIEW STRATEGIES:

- Re-visit your answers to the commonly asked questions. How could you make them better? Write your answers down or record yourself giving the answers. Use your primary way of operating – visual, auditory or kinaesthetic – to improve your efforts at remembering how to answer questions well.
- Practice with someone else. Ask a friend or family member to ask the commonly asked questions and the questions that you have created around a particular job. You could ask several friends or family members to form an interview panel and practice some more. Verbalising your responses is a great way of becoming used to responding aloud to questions. You will become better at it, the more you do that.
- What questions do you ask about the job or the company? Could they be better?
- Have you been guilty of asking questions about pay or annual leave? If so, make sure that you don't do that again. Those sorts of questions are best left until you know that they want you. You're in a better bargaining position at that time.
- Think about how you behave at the end of the interview. Is there anything you can do to leave the interviewers with a more favourable view of you? Do you shake theirs hands with a firm grip while looking at them in the eyes? Do you thank them for the opportunity to meet with them?

WHAT IF YOU THINK YOU'VE PERFORMED WELL IN THE INTERVIEW, BUT THEY GO COLD AFTERWARDS?

My first response to this is that it is likely that at least one of your referees is not providing the positive reference that you would expect.

You could call each of your referees and ask them what sort of things they have been asked. You should get some sort of idea from their responses as long as you keep it free of emotion and fairly conversational.

Alternatively, you could ask a friend or family member to call your referee and pretend that they are someone from a business or agency seeking a verbal reference from that person. The person who does this for you will need to sound professional and know the sort of questions that a referee will be asked. Again, make sure that they keep the emotion out of this and don't say anything in anger to your referee. After all, they're just on a fact-finding mission to determine that your referees are saying positive things about you.

If you discover that one of your referees is not being positive, approach someone else and ask if they will be your referee. Insert their details on your resume and delete the less positive person's details. Don't contact the 'less than positive person' to give them a piece of your mind. You never know what contacts a potential employer might have and you don't want to have 'burnt your bridges' by acting out of anger.

Another reason that an employer/recruiter might go cold afterwards might be nothing to do with you but a whole lot to do with that person's or company's poor communication systems or internal processes.

They might not have a practice for getting back to people they've interviewed. That is a poor practice – but it happens. Remember that it has nothing to do with your worth as a person or as a candidate for a job!

HANDLING THE STRESS OF AN INTERVIEW

Some anxiety is normal when we have a job interview. We produce the adrenalin we need to encourage us to perform well. However, too much will kill our performance because our brain will be swamped by it and our thought processes will stall — just at the time when we need them to flow.

I know the stress of fronting up to an interview when you really need a job because you've got to feed the kids or make your car payment or pay the rent or all of those things. As well, I always feel more stressed when the job is one that I *really* want or one I've wanted for ages.

A certain level of stress actually helps our performance but too much stress leads to a decrease in our ability to perform well. That's when we find it hard to concentrate on the question we've just been asked and come up with a less than stellar answer.

The Yerkes-Dodson Law of stress and performance indicates that difficult or unfamiliar tasks require lower levels of arousal (or stress) for optimal performance. So, the more you can make the interview process less difficult and more familiar, the more likely you will be to be on the 'up-side' of the performance curve rather than the 'down-side'.

So, what can you do to make it less stressful? Prepare for the job interview. Work out what responses you're going to give to the commonly asked questions and practice — out loud — what your answers will be. Ask family members or friends to practice interviewing you. Become more familiar with the process. Listen to their feedback (as long as it's constructive).

Because we respond differently as individuals to stress, you might want to also incorporate mindfulness techniques into your preparation. Getting up a bit earlier on the morning of an interview and meditating, or doing something you know calms you down and has you be more centred, is worth considering.

Why do I think this is so important for job interviews? Well, it's not just about you!

When you are feeling <u>very</u> stressed, the interviewer senses your stress. They are impacted by it and they might wonder what's wrong, why you are sitting there so uptight and tense. They, consciously or subconsciously, recoil from it. Their brain starts coming up with reasons you are not comfortable and engaged.

They might assume that you are not as competent as you seemed on paper. They might think that you will be someone who will bring stress and anxiety to their team, or that you will not handle stress well in your job. They might think you're trying to hide something. They will automatically make something up in their heads to explain why you're stressed. It's what we do as human beings.

You can see why your stress can be an issue. If your stress level is too high it creates a barrier to you being seen as a positive, confident candidate.

FINALLY, DON'T TAKE THE RESULTS OF THE INTERVIEW PERSONALLY.

It won't be personal to the interviewer. They're just interviewing people that have already jumped over the first hurdle and have made it to the final straight.

Getting the job – or not – has nothing to do with your worth as a person.

What it means is that you have got onto the racetrack because your written application worked. If you miss out, don't worry. You'll get onto another racetrack and have another go at winning the race.

CHAPTER TEN

LAST WORDS

THE KEY POINTS OF THIS BOOK

- Attitude is everything. Don't listen to negativity; focus on being positive.
- The two sets of skills involved in the job search process can be learned.
- If you're not getting interviews, completely review your written application.
- Create an achievements-based resume rather than having a boring old list of duties resume.
- If you're getting the interviews but not the jobs, review your preparation for the interviews.
- Practice, practice, practice. It really makes a difference to your performance and your results.
- You don't have to be an extravert to succeed.
- Preparation leads to confidence. Confidence leads to success.
- There are ways to conquer the nerves!

- Get your family or friends to help you. Work as a team.
- Treat your job search like a job. Be organised and keep it dynamic.
- It's not personal – whether you get the job or not.
- Get momentum going and keep it going.
- Expand your contacts list and work it!

I genuinely want you to succeed. I know that there are very few dole-bludgers out there (as they say in Australia) and that most people want to work.

Please take on board at least some of my suggestions and see what a difference it makes.

If you would like to provide feedback, please email me on landthatjobaftercovid19@gmail.com

APPENDICES

APPENDIX A
YOUR SKILLS

It is important to identify what skills you have so that you can write them down in your resume as well as confidently tell interviewers about them. Many people don't stop to analyse what skills they have and so they sell themselves short.

Qualify your skills by adding adverbs to show how well you do the skill. Check Appendix E for adverbs.

Be specific – writing 'good communication skills' is inadequate. What communication skills are you really good at? They're the ones to let the reader know about. Telling them that you are 'good at providing succinct and practical explanations about complex technical processes' is much more likely to get their attention! It gives them a lot more useful information about you.

Communication skills include writing, speaking and listening. If you're good at a specific form of writing (such as with technical material), say so. If you enjoy speaking to large groups of people, include that on your skills list. If you're a good listener, make sure that you let the employer know that. It's not a common skill!

Some people get communication and interpersonal skills mixed up. Interpersonal skills are to do with how well and in what way you relate to people. They can be broken down into more specific statements, too. See the next page.

SOME EXERCISES TO HELP CLARIFY YOUR SKILLS

Following are pages of skills but first here are some exercises you might like to tackle to really help you with working it all out:

1. Go through the lists on the following pages. Highlight or underline what skills you have before you start putting your resume together. Take your time and don't brush any aside. Even if you have a low level of a particular skill, highlight it.
2. Then circle the top ten skills that you like to use, even if some of them are not as developed as you would like. Those skills are the ones that need to go on your resume and, if they are not as developed as you would like, they are the skills that should be considered if you're thinking about further study.
3. Ask 6 people who know you well (family, friends) to tell you 6 <u>positive</u> skills that they believe you have. Don't prompt them. Just let them tell you. Write them down. You will probably be surprised at what they say. Don't argue with them either. They are letting you know what they observe. Add

any skills that you hadn't thought about to your list of key skills.
4. Google the skills required to do the sort of jobs you've had experience with or those you'd like to have. Note down those skills you already have.

SKILLS SUMMARY

This is just a summary of types of skills that people can have. On the next few pages, you will find lots of other skills as well. You might have highly specialized skills that belong with a specific industry. Add them in to the lists here.

Communication skills (can be broken down further)
- Writing (reports, technical, etc)
- Speaking (small, large groups, etc)
- Listening (to understand concepts or problems, etc)

Complex problem solving

Computer skills
- Competence with Microsoft Word, Excel, PowerPoint, Access
- Programming skills

Critical thinking
- Conceive and develop ideas

Customer service skills
- Effectively solve customer problems
- Negotiation
- Mediate

Decision making

Design
- An event, a product or a service
- Present your ideas to management

Engineering or mechanical skills
- Planning, assembling, operating

Event management
- Plan and coordinate event
- Delegate tasks
- Manage logistical and people issues

Financial management
- Create budgets
- Allocate resources
- Liaise across organisation

Interpersonal skills
- Collaboration
- Conflict management
- Establish rapport
- Interact effectively
- Team player/manager
- Negotiation

Leadership
- Initiate change
- Consult with staff
- Motivate others
- Managing teams

Maintain records
- Log data
- Collate & tabulate data
- Spreadsheets

Math skills
- Calculate
- Compute
- Organise
- Solve math problems

Monitoring or observing
- People, data or things

Planning Skills
- Defining goals & objectives
- Develop projects or programs
- Evaluation

Proof reading and editing
- Use company Style Guide
- Check for errors in wording & structure

Research
- Ability to identify sources of data
- Interpret information & identify most relevant data
- Present findings

Sales & marketing skills
- Promote goods or services
- Close sales

Team player
- Contribute ideas to group
- Achieve consensus
- Plan

Training skills
- Identify training needs
- Develop & deliver a training program
- Evaluate programs

SKILLS-FOCUSSED PHRASES TO USE ON YOUR RESUME – IN RANDOM ORDER

• Writes clearly and concisely • Listens attentively • Openly expresses ideas • Negotiates/resolves differences • Provides and asks for feedback • Offers well-thought-out solutions • Identifies and gathers appropriate resources • Thoroughly researches background information • Leads and directs others • Teaches/trains/instructs • Counsels/coaches • Manages conflict • Helps team members set and achieve goals • Delegates effectively • Manages social media campaigns • Measures and analyses campaign results • Identifies and connects with industry influencers • Sparks social conversation within the brand's community • Creates and executes content strategies • Drives engagement and leads • Enhances brand image through social presence • Establish realistic short and long-term goals and objectives • Organize and allocate the right resources for task achievement • Schedule and co-ordinate activities for maximum efficiency • Effectively work with diverse staff members • Empower staff members to achieve outcomes • Monitor progress towards desired objectives • Handle obstacles and challenges to goal achievement • Motivate staff towards goal attainment • Build constructive relationships with customers and team members • Recruit, place and develop staff • Manage and evaluate staff performance • Identify and resolve conflict • Develop and implement policies, practices and procedures for improvement	• Analytical thinking, planning • Strong verbal and personal communication skills • Accuracy and attention to details • Organization and prioritization skills • Problem analysis and ability to solve problems efficiently • An experienced team leader with the ability to initiate/manage cross-functional teams and multi-disciplinary projects • Critical thinking, decision-making and problem solving skills • Planning – events, workloads, strategy • Project management skills - influencing, leading, negotiating and delegating abilities • Conflict resolution • Ability to handle stressful situations • Manage and complete multiple tasks accurately and by deadline • Take and distribute minutes of meetings within established time frames • Display solid working knowledge of standard computer applications including MS Word, Excel, Outlook and PowerPoint • Draft correspondence and documents using good language and grammar skills • Plan and implement office procedures to improve efficiency • Collect and review information to generate reports • Handle queries and requests for information competently & promptly • Monitor and maintain office supplies and equipment • Communicate clearly and professionally with internal and external customers • Work effectively as part of a team to achieve established outcomes • Maintain confidentiality and discretion • Basic/well-developed bookkeeping skills • Prepare accurate financial statements • Interpret financial statements and other accounting reports • Compile and analyse financial data to generate reports • Develop efficient financial reporting mechanisms • Plan and implement accounting controls

- Plan and implement change effectively
- Schedule sales and marketing activity
- Identify and assess customer needs
- Use products and services to resolve customer problems
- Plan and deliver presentations
- Handle customer objections effectively
- Negotiate to a win-win outcome
- Close the sale in a professional manner
- Manage all steps of the sales cycle effectively
- Conduct in-depth market research and analysis
- Track industry trends and competitor activity
- Identify and target new business
- Expand customer base or sales territory
- Provide excellent service to existing customer base
- Improve customer retention rates and sales
- Collaborate with all stakeholders to achieve targets and quotas
- Management skills – financial, project, change, people, strategic, technical, operational – don't just use these headings; include the specific skills within those areas
- Complex/multi-faceted problem solving
- Accurate cash handling skills
- Effective management of customer complaints
- Excellent customer service skills
- Inventory management
- Good visual merchandising skills
- Sound product knowledge
- Ability to establish rapport quickly & easily
- Accurate shift scheduling	- Implement and monitor new accounting practices
- Review and upgrade existing systems to improve efficiency
- Evaluate and communicate financial information
- Analyse and resolve accounting issues
- Control and report on expenditure
- Work cooperatively with the team to achieve objectives
- Liaise with regulators and external auditors
- Plan, forecast and administer the budget
- Supervise daily accounting operations
- Organize, co-ordinate and streamline workflow
- Keep up to date with current issues and changes in industry regulations
- Ensure strict adherence to regulations, procedures and practices
- Ability to develop a concept through to a well-documented design
- Excellent management skills
- Ability to lead and supervise the individuals to increase the level of productivity
- Ability to solve the ongoing issues or defects
- Engineering - aerospace, biomedical, chemical, civil, computer, electrical, electronic, genetic, mechanical, nuclear, software, structural, systems, etc – get specific about the skills within each of these fields
- Good public speaking skills
- Sound writing skills – understanding of audience and formal/informal styles
- Well-developed research skills
- Ability to effectively interpret and evaluate complex information
- Sound typography skills
- Excellent print design & layout skills

SKILLS SPECIFIC TO TECHNOLOGY AND COMPUTERS

- Utilize technology to effectively support the management function
- Coding
- Development Operations (DevOps)
- Mobile development
- Social Media Expertise
- Agile Methodology
- Experience with Emerging Technologies
- SQL – structured query language
- Expertise in Java Development and Object-Oriented Analysis/Design
- Understand the potential of Java technology
- Cybersecurity
- Big Data Analytics
- User Experience Design	- Create and maintain accurate databases
- Retrieve information quickly and efficiently
- Familiar with industry-specific software like Xero, Great Plains, QuickBooks, Peachtree, SAP and tax preparation software
- Languages- C, C++, JAVA, Javascript
- Operating Systems- Window 95/98/2000 NT, UNIX, MVS
- Internet Technologies- CSS, XSL, XML, HTML, XHTML
- Software- Adobe Acrobat Professional (PDF), MS Office (Word, Excel, Access, PowerPoint), etc.
- Content Management- Oracle ProtalsAS, Oracle Universal Content Manager, etc.
- Database Application- Lotus Notes, Oracle RDBMS, etc.

Remember that it's important to indicate how well you perform these skills. See the appendix on adverbs.

YOUR TOP SKILLS

Write down the skills that you love to use, that you're good at, and the ones that don't feel like 'work'.

Review them annually in case you've stumbled upon a skill that you LOVE to use. It happens!

1	
2	
3	
4	
5	
6	
7	
8	
9	
10	

ern
APPENDIX B
YOUR ATTRIBUTES/ PERSONAL CHARACTERISTICS

ATTRIBUTES/ PERSONAL CHARACTERISTICS LIST

Active	Efficient	Persistent
Adaptable	Empathetic listener	Persevering
Adventurous	Energetic	Persuasive
Alert	Enthusiastic	Polite
Ambitious	Enterprising	Positive
Amiable	Establish rapport with others	Practical
Amusing	Fair	Precise
Analytical	Flexible and adaptable	Proactive
Articulate	Focused	Problem solver
Assertive	Friendly	Process oriented
Attention to detail	Generous	Productive
Attentive	Gregarious	Professional
Balanced	Happy	Quick-witted
Brave	Hardworking	Quiet
Bright	Helpful	Rational
Business-like	Honest	Realistic
Calm	Imaginative	Reliable
Capable	Impartial	Resourceful
Careful	Independent	Responsible
Cheerful	Industrious	Results driven
Clear-headed	Innovative	Results oriented
Communicative	Insightful	Self-confident
Compassionate	Intelligent	Self-disciplined
Competent	Intuitive	Self-reliant
Confident	Inventive	Sensible
Conscientious	Keen to 'get it right'	Sincere
Considerate	Kind	Straightforward
Consistent	Lateral thinker	Strong
Cooperative	Leader	Team player
Courageous	Logical	Thoughtful
Creative	Loyal	Tidy
Decisive	Methodical	Thorough
Dedicated	Modest	Tolerant
Dependable	Motivated	Trustworthy
Determined	Neat	Understanding
Diligent	Optimistic	Versatile
Diplomatic	Organised	Warm
Disciplined	Outgoing	Well organised
Discreet	Passionate	Willing
Dynamic	Patient	Wise
Easy going	People-oriented	Witty
Effective		

YOUR TOP ATTRIBUTES/ PERSONAL CHARACTERISTICS

Write down the attributes that you are most proud of - or the ones people comment on the most frequently.

From your list, select the attributes/ personal characteristics that you think an employer would most want to see on your resume. Include about three of them on your resume.

1	
2	
3	
4	
5	
6	
7	
8	
9	
10	

APPENDIX C
YOUR VALUES

While you would not usually put your values on your resume, it would be wise of you to identify just what values are important to you.

Identifying your values can help you know whether you are in the right sort of job role; your self-awareness will increase; and you will have more clarity about whether you are living your life in a way that's consistent with those values.

Employers usually look favourably on prospective employees who know themselves well and can articulate what's important to them.

Businesses often write their values on their website. You should note down those you have in common with the business prior to going to an interview and use that information at an opportune time. If they don't have them written there, look at the language they use on their website to determine what values they appear to hold.

Go through the following list and highlight or underline all of the values that are important to you.

Afterwards, select the ten that are the most important to you and write them in the table at the end of this appendix.

YOUR VALUES

Accountability	Environmentalism	Outdoors
Accuracy	Ethics	Outrageousness
Achievement	Excellence	Partnership
Adaptability	Excitement	Patience
Advancement	Experience	Passion
Adventurous	Expertise	Peace
Agility	Exploration	Perfection
Altruism	Expressiveness	Perseverance
Ambition	Fairness	Persistence
Approachability	Faith	Persuasiveness
Assertiveness	Fame	Philanthropy
Attractiveness	Family	Poise
Audacity	Fashion	Popularity
Awareness	Fearlessness	Power
Balanced	Financial independence	Practicality
Being the best	Fitness	Pragmatism
Belonging	Flexibility	Precision
Boldness	Fluency	Privacy
Bravery	Focus	Professionalism
Brilliance	Fortune	Punctuality
Calmness	Frankness	Qualifications
Candor	Freedom	Quickness
Certainty	Friendship	Rationality
Challenge	Frugality	Recognition
Change	Fun	Reflection
Charity	Gallantry	Reliability
Charm	Generosity	Reputation
Chastity	Giving	Resilience
Cheerfulness	Grace	Resourcefulness
Clarity	Gratitude	Resolve
Cleanliness	Growth	Respect
Clear-mindedness	Guidance	Responsibility
Cleverness	Happiness	Sacrifice
Comfort	Harmony	Satisfaction
Commitment	Health	Security
Community	Helpfulness	Selflessness
Compassion	Heroism	Self-respect
Competence	Honesty	Serenity
Competition	Honour	Sexuality
Concentration	Humility	Sharing
Confidence	Humour	Simplicity
Congruence	Hygiene	Sincerity
Connection	Imagination	Solitude
Consistency	Impartiality	Spirituality
Contribution	Impeccability	Spontaneity
Control	Independence	Stability
Cooperation	Individuality	Status
Creativity	Inspiration	Strength
Credibility	Integrity	Structure

Curiosity	Intelligence	Success
Daring	Intuition	Support
Decisiveness	Joy	Surprise
Dependability	Justice	Sympathy
Depth	Kindness	Synergy
Determination	Knowledge	Tactfulness
Devotion	Leadership	Teaching
Dignity	Learning	Teamwork
Diligence	Logic	Thoroughness
Direction	Love	Thoughtfulness
Discipline	Loyalty	Tidiness
Discretion	Making a difference	Traditionalism
Discernment	Mastery	Trust
Diversity	Maturity	Truth
Drive	Mindfulness	Understanding
Duty	Moderation	Uniqueness
Dynamism	Modesty	Unity
Economy	Money	Usefulness
Education	Motivation	Variety
Effectiveness	Neatness	Victory
Efficiency	Nerve	Vision
Elegance	Nonconformity	Vitality
Empathy	Obedience	Warm-heartedness
Encouragement	Open-mindedness	Wealth
Energy	Optimism	Winning
Enjoyment	Order	Wisdom
Entertainment	Organization	Worthiness
Enthusiasm	Originality	Zeal

YOUR TOP VALUES

Write down the values that are the most important to you. Review them every couple of years. Our values don't usually change all that much but can change when our life circumstances change. For example, people usually look at things differently after they travel, when they have babies, and when those babies grow up and leave home.

1	
2	
3	
4	
5	
6	
7	
8	
9	
10	

APPENDIX D
ADJECTIVES

Adjectives are words that describe things, and they are useful in providing further information about you to a prospective employer. They show the reader what level of competence that you have with particular skills. Obviously, you need to be honest about the level of competence you have.

Some examples are:

- **Excellent** report writing skills
- **Sound** knowledge of software design
- **Good** problem solving ability

The list in this appendix is for you to use as a prompt when you are writing your resume and application letters.

ADJECTIVES LIST

Accountable	Easy-going	Likeable	Resilient
Accurate	Electronic	Local	Resourceful
Adaptable	Eloquent	Loyal	Responsible
Adept	Emergent	Mature	Responsive
Advanced	Energetic Enthusiastic	Measured	Secure
Approachable	Exact	Mentored	Sincere
Capable	Excellent	Methodical	Sociable
Committed	Expert	Motivated	Sophisticated
Competitive	Fair	Negotiated	Sound
Confident	Faithfull	Optimistic	Strong
Conscientious	Flexible	Orderly	Succinct
Constructive	Frank	Organised	Superior
Cooperative	Generous	Passionate	Systematic
Creative	Global	Permanent	Tactful
Decisive	Good	Persistent	Tenacious
Determine	Guide	Personable	Thorough
Design	Happy	Pleasant	Thoughtful
Detailed	Honest	Positive	Timely
Dexterous	Imaginative	Pro-active	Unified
Diligent	Impartial	Productive	Unique
Discreet	Industrious	Prompt	Valiant
Diverse	Influential	Punctual	Versatile
Driven	Keen	Purposeful	Warm
Dynamic	Kind	Realistic	Willing
Eager	Knowledgeable	Reliable	World-class

APPENDIX E
ADVERBS

Adverbs show <u>how</u> you do something. They support the verb and qualify how well or in what manner you do things.

Many adverbs end in -ly. Some examples are:

Thoughtfully responded to complaints

Accurately recorded data

Quickly completed tasks

Knowing that you can perform tasks quickly, carefully or accurately provides the prospective employer with added information about you.

When job seekers just provide employers with lists of tasks that they have done in previous roles, the employer has no idea whether they were done competently or not. When you write down how well you did things, the employer is more likely to be impressed with your application.

ADVERBS LIST

Accurately	Faithfully	Resourcefully
Actively	Gladly	Responsibly
Ambitiously	Honestly	Significantly
Analytically	Imaginatively	Soundly
Artistically	Independently	Steadily
Assertively	Logically	Strongly
Carefully	Meticulously	Substantially
Competently	Patiently	Successfully
Competitively	Practically	Succinctly
Conscientiously	Precisely	Supportively
Cooperatively	Professionally	Tactfully
Creatively	Proficiently	Technically
Diligently	Progressively	Thoroughly
Effectively	Quickly	Thoughtfully
Efficiently	Rationally	Truthfully
Energetically	Reliably	Voluntarily
Enthusiastically	Realistically	Warmly

APPENDIX F
LINKS TO MY YOUTUBE VIDEOS

Why Employers Ask the Questions they Do?

https://www.youtube.com/watch?v=rMSYsn-oHFI&t=5s

Recruitment Services: what to say and how to approach them

https://www.youtube.com/watch?v=lFVoeut_Svo

Technology in Recruitment

https://www.youtube.com/watch?v=s8OoL73L30s&t=1s

How to Stop being Nervous in Job Interviews

https://www.youtube.com/watch?v=l38-bYO0EEo&t=12s

How to answer Tricky Job Interview Questions

https://www.youtube.com/watch?v=k9t-QHqj3zc&t=6s

How to Succeed at Job Interviews

https://www.youtube.com/watch?v=1mYM4PiddJI&t=27s

How to Get a Job

https://www.youtube.com/watch?v=GN1n5y-eEzY&t=5s

Work Has Changed

https://www.youtube.com/watch?v=ld1diKAlIRQ

Looking at Careers Differently

https://www.youtube.com/watch?v=QrmmzRKJEiw

Creating a Career Plan

https://www.youtube.com/watch?v=db4JrsJ-aS4&t=5s

APPENDIX G
SOME COMMON MISTAKES MADE WHEN WRITING EMAILS, LETTERS AND RESUMES

Your – means it belongs to them Example: Your coffee is in the cup.
You're – an abbreviation of 'you are' Example: You're good at making coffee.

THIS IS A VERY COMMON MISTAKE. PLEASE CHECK THAT YOU HAVEN'T MADE IT!

———

Their – means it belongs to them Example: Their coffee is awesome.
They're – an abbreviation of 'they are'Example: They're going to have coffee now.
There – a place, such as 'over there' Example: I don't want to go there for coffee.

———

Two – a number. Example: I've had two cups of coffee today.

To – indicating direction or part of a verb. Example: I'm going to get a coffee now.

Too – in addition, or excessive. Example: You can never have too many coffees.

———

'**A lot**' is written as two words. '**Thank you**' is written as two words.

———

Increasingly I have seen people write 'a part' incorrectly. It changes the meaning significantly.

'**A part**' means a section of something. Example: The core is a part of the apple.

'**Apart**' means being separate from someone. Example: I hate being apart from my boyfriend.

———

'**Could've**' **is the abbreviation of 'could have'**. Therefore, don't write 'could of'. It's incorrect.

It's the same with '**should've**'. It's the abbreviation of 'should have'.

(I think people make the assumption that it's 'of' because of the sound it makes.)

———

Apostrophes:

If it's a plural, it doesn't need an apostrophe. For example, apples, cars, CDs – don't need apostrophes

An apostrophe is needed if you want to abbreviate 'it is' – becomes it's

Example: It's ages since I had a cup of coffee.

An apostrophe is <u>not needed</u> if you say, 'The cat was licking its paw'.

(It's an example of how the English language is inconsistent. Normally the possessive is marked by an apostrophe, but an exception is with 'its').

———

While you might think that I've got too fussy here, remember that this matters to some employers and you might not make it to the interview stage if your application is littered with what they will see as mistakes. They will make the assumption that you have been too lazy to proof-read your application; that your attention to detail is poor; or worse, that you're ignorant. **The employer needs to know that they can trust you to produce written information that is grammatically correct. They don't want to look bad.**

SPECIAL OFFER FROM SHARON LUXFORD, LINKEDIN EXPERT

Hey Everyone

I hope you have enjoyed reading this book and got something out of every section that you can implement to get that job you want.

If you would like to join my LinkedIn network, simply follow these 3 Steps.

1. Find me on LinkedIn and send me a connection request.
2. Personalising the request to connect with a message...because you know that it will stand out...tell me about one thing you are going to change about your LinkedIn Profile.
3. Respond to my 'acceptance message' when you receive it.

SPECIAL OFFER

If you would like a **'One Hour LinkedIn Intensive Coaching Call'** that will be all about you and how you can tell your story, bring out our key skills and achievements and articulate your value to a prospective employer, I am offering a $AU50 discount off the usual price of $AU350.

If you would like to take advantage of this offer, please message me on LinkedIn to arrange a free 5 minute initial chat.

Dear reader,

We hope you enjoyed reading *Land That Job*. Please take a moment to leave a review, even if it's a short one. Your opinion is important to us.

Discover more books by Sharon Davey at https://www.nextchapter.pub/authors/sharon-davey

Want to know when one of our books is free or discounted? Join the newsletter at http://eepurl.com/bqqB3H

Best regards,

Sharon Davey and the Next Chapter Team

ABOUT THE AUTHOR

Sharon Davey was born in Mildura, Victoria, Australia, and is the eldest child of hard-working farmers, both now deceased.

Post-school, she had a number of unskilled jobs ranging from grape-picking to bank clerk to waitressing. She didn't really find any lasting satisfaction with any of them. A couple of major life events (father's death, her divorce) occurred, and Sharon took stock of her life. She decided she needed to make some changes.

Remembering her primary teacher's wish of wanting to see her on the teachers' register one day, she went back to school and then university to become a secondary school teacher. Sharon characteristically threw herself into teaching and took up a range of positions within her school. When she was asked by her principal to take up the careers' teacher position at her school, she did so with an open mind and unexpectedly fell in love with the role. Sharon went on to complete a Graduate Diploma in Career Education.

She has held many positions of responsibility within the careers field, including a state-wide responsibility for career education and work experience for schools. She was the President of the Career Education Association of Victoria and on the Executive

Committee of the (then) Australian Association of Careers Counsellors in the 1990s. Sharon has delivered workshops and spoken at many careers' events. Sharon has worked in private and government schools, in TAFEs (community colleges) and for universities.

Sharon has also managed an employment service for a not-for-profit organisation and grew the community education offerings for Family Planning Victoria. Sharon also had the roles of Client Services Manager for a disability organisation, and a writer of policies and procedures for another not-for-profit organisation. She has added to her list of job roles with editing, coaching, speaking and being the chair of a small disability charity.

Over her career, and intertwined with her other roles, Sharon has provided careers counselling and job search assistance to thousands of people across all age groups.

She is known for her warmth, sense of humour, intelligence, and her dedication to encouraging others to recognise and act on their potential.

Sharon spends her time between Melbourne, Victoria, and the Gold Coast, Queensland, in Australia.

Land That Job
ISBN: 978-4-86747-736-6
Mass Market

Published by
Next Chapter
1-60-20 Minami-Otsuka
170-0005 Toshima-Ku, Tokyo
+818035793528

24th May 2021

www.ingramcontent.com/pod-product-compliance
Lightning Source LLC
LaVergne TN
LVHW032008070526
838202LV00059B/6355